Flight Deck

US Navy Carrier Operations 1940-1945

By Al Adcock

Color by Don Greer and Andrew Probert

squadron/signal publications

ISBN 0-89747-441-4

If you have any photographs of aircraft, armor, soldiers or ships of any nation, particularly wartime snapshots, why not share them with us and help make Squadron/Signal's books all the more interesting and complete in the future. Any photograph sent to us will be copied and the original returned. The donor will be fully credited for any photos used. Please send them to:

Squadron/Signal Publications, Inc.
1115 Crowley Drive
Carrollton, TX 75011-5010

Если у вас есть фотографии самолетов, вооружения, солдат или кораблей любой страны, особенно, снимки времен войны, поделитесь с нами и помогите сделать новые книги издательства Эскадрон/Сигнал еще интереснее. Мы переснимем ваши фотографии и вернем оригиналы. Имена приславших снимки будут сопровождать все опубликованные фотографии. Пожалуйста, присылайте фотографии по адресу:

Squadron/Signal Publications, Inc.
1115 Crowley Drive
Carrollton, TX 75011-5010

軍用機、装甲車両、兵士、軍艦などの写真を所持しておられる方はいらっしゃいませんか？どの国のものでも結構です。作戦中に撮影されたものが特に良いのです。Squadron/Signal社の出版する刊行物において、このような写真は内容を一層充実し、興味深くすることができます。当方にお送り頂いた写真は、複写の後お返しいたします。出版物中に写真を使用した場合は、必ず提供者のお名前を明記させて頂きます。お写真は下記にご送付ください。

Squadron/Signal Publications, Inc.
1115 Crowley Drive
Carrollton, TX 75011-5010

(Cover) Grumman F6F-3 Hellcat fighters are prepared for launch from USS COWPENS (CVL-25) in January of 1944. The INDEPEN-DENCE class light carrier operated with Task Group 58.3 during US raids on the Marshall Islands. The air attacks softened Japanese defenses on the Marshalls prior to the US invasion the following month. (Elsilrac)

Photo Credits

All of the photos in this publication are Official US Navy Photographs that have been declassified and made available by the following photo archivists:

Real War Photos	George Chizmar
Elsilrac	Bob Carlisle
Floating Drydock	Tom Walkowiak
National Archives	Naval History Center
Paul Durand	Museum of Naval History
Jim Sullivan	Kim Chetwyn

A very special thanks to fellow Squadron author Jim Sullivan for loaning me some of his extensive collection of carrier deck photos from the World War Two era.

Dedication:

In memory of Cmdr. Will W. 'Dub' Taylor, US Navy World War Two Ace and First Class flight instructor.

(Previous Page) Lt. Cdr. Albert B. Cahn gives the take-off signal to a Grumman TBM-1C Avenger aboard USS SAN JACINTO (CVL-30) during exercises on 16 May 1944. The Avenger torpedo bomber was assigned to Torpedo Squadron 51 (VT-51) aboard SAN JACINTO, one of nine INDEPENDENCE class light carriers to see service during World War Two. Among VT-51's pilots in this period was Lt. George H. W. Bush, the future 41st President of the United States. (US Navy)

Introduction

An aircraft carrier's flight deck has often been described as choreographed chaos and one of the most dangerous places to work. United States Navy flight and deck crews had their hands full just trying to stay alive during World War Two. This was due to bad weather, rain slicked decks, turning propellers, highly volatile aviation fuel, bombs, rockets, and out of control aircraft landing on the flight deck. Add to those elements enemy bombs, strafing aircraft, and the dreaded *kamikaze* ('divine wind;' Japanese suicide attackers) and it is a wonder that anyone on the flight deck made it home alive; many crewmen did not survive. This photo monograph illustrates their story.

Carrier aviation humbly began on 10 November 1910, when aviation pioneer Eugene Ely flew his Curtiss D-IV pusher biplane off a flight deck constructed on the cruiser **USS BIRMINGHAM** (CL-2) in the fall of 1910. After making a successful landing at Norfolk, Virginia, Ely immediately began trying to convince the USN to let him attempt to land his small aircraft onto the deck of a ship. A far seeing person in the Navy gave the go ahead and a flight deck 32 feet (9.8 M) wide and 130 feet (39.6 M) long was constructed on the armored cruiser **USS PENNSYLVANIA** (ACR-4). Twenty-two ropes with sandbags attached at each end would assist in arresting the Curtiss, which was equipped with three pairs of hooks to catch the ropes. On 18 January 1911, swooping in low over San Francisco Bay, Ely approached and made an arrested landing on the converted armored cruiser. Carrier aviation had come closer to reality.

Ely's feat drew some attention in naval circles around the world and a few countries, namely Britain and Japan, began studying how to encompass the new technology into their navies. The US Navy's first aircraft carrier was the **USS LANGLEY** (CV-1), the converted collier **JUPITER** (AC-3). The LANGLEY was commissioned in 1922 and embarked Vought **VE-7SF** fighters, which were equipped with arresting hooks and strengthened landing gear. The LANGLEY was converted into a seaplane tender (AV-3) in 1937 and lost in action off Java on 27 February 1942.

In 1922, the US began converting the battle cruisers **LEXINGTON** (CC-1) and **SARATOGA** (CC-3) into aircraft carriers. (This conversion was a result of the 1922 Washington Naval Treaty, which limited the strengths of the world's major navies of the time.) The new carriers were designated CV-2 and CV-3, respectively, and both were commissioned in 1927. The LEXINGTON and SARATOGA began operating Martin **T4M-1** torpedo bombers and Boeing **F2B-1** fighters from their decks.

The US commissioned **RANGER** (CV-4) – the first US ship designed from the keel up as an aircraft carrier – in 1934. She began embarking Boeing **F4B-1** fighters and Great Lakes **BG-1** dive-bombers. The BG-1 operated from RANGER until 1938 and with the US Marines until 1940. The Boeing F4Bs were superceded in service by the portly Grumman fighters. This line began with the Grumman **FF-1**, which entered service in 1933, followed by the **F2F** in 1935 and the **F3F** one year later. These Grumman biplanes led to the **F4F Wildcat** monoplane, which entered US Navy service in late 1940.

Pre-World War Two carrier aircraft were colorfully marked with carrier air wing colors painted on the tails and Chrome Yellow (FS13538) wing upper surfaces. Each squadron had six sections – three aircraft per section – which were assigned a color for the upper wing chevrons. Section leaders' aircraft displayed an aft fuselage band and cowl band, while the second and third aircraft in each section had the upper or lower cowl band painted, respectively. Fabric covered aircraft surfaces

A Boeing F3B-1, Black 9 from Fighting Squadron Two (VF-2), launches from USS LEXINGTON (CV-2) sometime in the late 1920s. Hooks on a crossbar mounted on the landing gear strut provided a back-up arresting gear system. LEXINGTON and her sister SARATOGA (CV-3) were originally fitted with both longitudinal (fore-and-aft) and transverse arresting cables. The longitudinal cables were removed in 1930. The F3B was painted in an overall Light Gray (FS16376) scheme with a Lemon Yellow (FS13655) tail. F3Bs served in US Navy front-line fighter squadrons between 1928 and 1932. Twin 8-inch (20.3 cM) gun turrets were mounted in front of LEXINGTON's superstructure; a second pair were mounted aft of the stack. (Real War Photos)

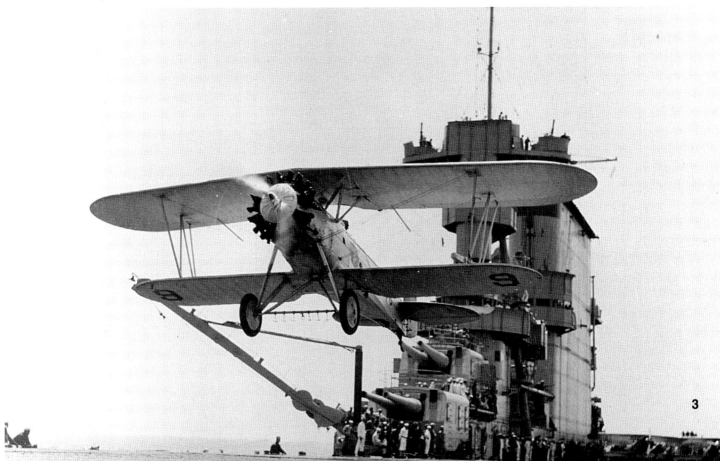

A Martin T4M (1-T-14) from Torpedo Squadron One, Battle Force (VT-1B) is spotted on LEXINGTON's flight deck. (The US Navy's Battle Force between the World Wars consisted of the carriers and other frontline strike elements.) The outer wing bays folded back to decrease storage space aboard the carrier. The T4M was a torpedo bomber with a top speed of 114 MPH (183.5 KMH) and a range of 350 miles (563.3 KM) while armed with a torpedo. This aircraft equipped torpedo squadrons aboard LEXINGTON and SARATOGA between 1928 and 1937. The tail unit color was Lemon Yellow (FS13655), while the upper wing was Chrome Yellow (FS13538) and the crankcase cover was Willow Green (FS14187). (Real War Photos)

A Vought O2U-2 Corsair from Scouting Squadron Two, Battle Force (VS-2B) approaches LEXINGTON with its tail hook down in April of 1930. The O2U-2 could be configured for either carrier, floatplane, or landplane use. Bomb racks were fitted to the lower wings. The tail color for LEXINGTON's aircraft was Lemon Yellow. (Real War Photos)

were finished in Aluminum Dope (FS27178). Metal surfaces were painted either Aluminum or Light Gray (FS16376) to protect against corrosion caused by salty sea spray. These bright colors were not exactly camouflage, but were more akin to bird plumage. The colors also provided for safety over water and unit identification.

By 1941, the US commissioned three more carriers: **YORKTOWN** (CV-5), **ENTERPRISE** (CV-6), and **WASP** (CV-7). **HORNET** (CV-8) was nearing completion for commissioning in the fall of 1941. Aircraft development kept pace with construction of the new carriers and two monoplanes – the Douglas **TBD Devastator** torpedo bomber and the **Brewster F2A** Buffalo fighter – began operations with the fleet in 1937 and 1940, respectively. War was being waged around the world in 1940, with the Japanese and Germans attacking their neighbors in Asia, Europe, and Africa. The US would soon be embroiled in this worldwide conflict.

A Boeing F4B-4 (3-F-7, BuNo 9256) from Fighting Squadron Three (VF-3) is parked on an outrigger aboard RANGER (CV-4) in the mid 1930s. The outriggers were used to free up deck space during flight operations. The tail is Willow Green and the Third Section leader's fuselage stripe is True Blue (FS15102). VF-3's insignia was painted on the fuselage side under the windshield. The F4B-4 could be configured as a fighter-bomber with the addition of underwing bomb racks for two 116 pound (52.6 KG) bombs. (Real War Photos)

A Grumman J2F-1 Duck (BuNo 0169) is raised to the flight deck on the amidships elevator of USS YORKTOWN (CV-5) on 2 November 1937. The J2F is aircraft number 4 of the ship's utility unit. This aircraft was finished overall Light Gray (FS16376), with the top of the upper wing in Chrome Yellow. The lower wing, the upper wing's undersurface, and the tail were finished in Aluminum Dope (FS27178). The rudder was stripped (front to back) Insignia Blue (FS15042), White (FS17875), and Insignia Red (FS11136). The J2F amphibian entered US Navy service in 1937 and served throughout World War Two. (National Archives)

Carrier Wing Tail Colors, July of 1937 through December of 1940

Carrier	Color (FS Number)
USS LEXINGTON (CV-2)	Lemon Yellow (FS13655)
USS SARATOGA (CV-3)	White (FS17875)
USS RANGER (CV-4)	Willow Green (FS14187)
USS YORKTOWN (CV-5)	Insignia Red (FS11136)
USS ENTERPRISE (CV-6)	True Blue (FS15102)
USS WASP (CV-7)	Black (FS17038)

Utility and Marine aircraft assigned to carriers had Aluminum tails with rudders striped (fore to aft) Insignia Red, White, and Insignia Blue (FS15042).

Squadron Section Colors

Section (Aircraft in Section)	Color (FS Number)
First (1-2-3)	Insignia Red (FS11136)
Second (4-5-6)	White (FS17875)
Third (7-8-9)	True Blue (FS15102)
Fourth (10-11-12)	Black (FS17038)
Fifth (13-14-15)	Willow Green (FS14187)
Sixth (16-17-18)	Lemon Yellow (FS13655)

The first aircraft in each section had the entire cowl band and an aft fuselage band painted in the section color. The second aircraft in the section had only the upper cowl in the section color, while the third aircraft in the section had only the lower cowl in the section color. All aircraft had upper wing chevrons in their section colors.

A Grumman F2F-1 (5-F-2, BuNo 9664) of Fighting Squadron Five (VF-5) sits on YORKTOWN's flight deck during a lull in flight operations during Fleet Problem XX in February of 1939. The upper wing top surfaces are Chrome Yellow and the tails are Insignia Red – the color assigned to the YORKTOWN Air Group. Metal surfaces were painted Light Gray, while fabric-covered wing surfaces were Aluminum Dope. A gun camera was mounted atop the upper wings of these Grumman fighters. The camera was used to confirm simulated 'kills' during peacetime training. The F2F-1 was armed with two .30 caliber (7.62MM) machine guns in the upper fuselage. The aircraft had a maximum speed of 231 MPH (371.7 KMH) at 7500 feet (2286 M) and a maximum range of 985 miles (1585.2 KM). (National Archives)

5

A Vought O3U-3 Corsair (BuNo 9147) launches from USS WASP (CV-7) during the ship's sea trials in 1939. The obsolete O3U-3 was part of WASP's utility unit and served as an observation trainer for the scouting squadron. This aircraft had a single bomb rack fitted to each of the lower wings. The finish is overall Aluminum with Chrome Yellow upper wing top surfaces and an Insignia Blue, White, and Insignia Red striped rudder. The O3U Corsair – derived from the earlier O2U – entered US Navy service in 1930. O3Us were the primary scout and observation aircraft on US capital ships during most of the 1930s. (Real War Photos)

A Douglas TBD-1 Devastator from Torpedo Squadron Three (VT-3) gets the cut signal from the Landing Signal Officer (LSO) as the plane approaches the flight deck of the SARATOGA (CV-3) in 1939. The arresting cables ('wires') were raised from the flight deck by 'fiddle bars,' which allowed the arresting hook to engage a cable. (The bars resembled the bridge that raised the strings over a fiddle's body.) The TBD was configured as a level bomber with a pair of bomb racks mounted on the fuselage stations. The Devastator was the first monoplane torpedo-bomber to enter US Navy service, with the first examples delivered to VT-3 on 5 October 1937. The TBD's maximum speed was 206 MPH (331.5 KMH) at 8000 feet (2438.4 M), while her range with a 1000 pound (453.6 KG) bomb was 716 miles (1152.3 KM). (National Archives)

A Douglas TBD-1 (5-T-11, BuNo 0284) from Torpedo Squadron Five (VT-5) crashed into the YORKTOWN's starboard catwalk on 3 September 1940. The pilot was Electrician's Mate First Class (Naval Aviation Pilot) C.M. O'Brien. The tail was Insignia Red and the top of the cowl was Black (FS17038), which indicated the second aircraft of VT-5's Fourth Section. This Devastator was repaired and ultimately assigned to Torpedo Squadron Eight (VT-8) aboard USS HORNET (CV-8). This aircraft and its crew was lost during the Battle of Midway on 4 June 1942. (National Archives)

A Northrop BT-1 (5-B-14, BuNo 0614) goes into the starboard cat-walk during a landing incident aboard YORKTOWN in 1940. The fire suppression crew in asbestos suits and other flight deck personnel rush to assist the flight crew. The BT-1's tail was Insignia Red and the top of the engine cowl was Willow Green for the Fifth Section's second aircraft. The BT-1 dive-bomber was the forerunner to the Douglas SBD Dauntless; Jack Northrop designed both aircraft. The maximum speed at 9500 feet (2895.6 M) was 222 MPH (357.3 KMH) and its range was 1150 miles (1850.7 KM). The BT-1 carried a 1000 pound bomb under the fuselage. YORKTOWN's VB-5 was the first unit to receive BT-1s in April of 1938. The BT-1 was replaced by the SBD in 1941 and was used for training and utility duties until 1943. (National Archives)

1941 – The US Goes to War

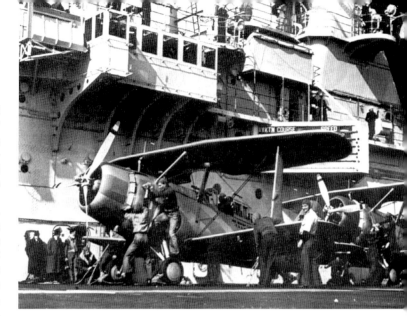

The year 1941 'came in like a lamb and out like a lion' for the US Navy. The US carriers in the Atlantic continued the 'neutrality patrols' begun the year before. These patrols escorted merchant convoys from the United States and Canada to Britain. The convoys were sent to reinforce that beleaguered island, which stood alone against the Nazis. US forces in the Atlantic carried a mandate to sink any ship or submarine that attacked these convoys.

The carriers RANGER (CV-4), YORKTOWN (CV-5), WASP (CV-7), and HORNET (CV-8), along with their escorts, sailed the Atlantic until the end of 1941, when the YORKTOWN was transferred to the Pacific. The RANGER's air group consisted of the Vought **SB2U Vindicator** scout bomber, the Grumman F4F Wildcat fighter, and the Douglas TBD Devastator torpedo bomber. YORKTOWN embarked the Curtiss **SBC Helldiver** biplane scout bomber, the F4F, and the TBD. WASP's air group was formed around the F4F, the SB2U, and the TBD. While the newly commissioned HORNET was undergoing training and work-up prior to her assignment to the Pacific, her air group consisted of the SBC, F4F, TBD, and the Brewster-designed Naval Aircraft Factory **SBN** scout bomber.

The US carriers in the Pacific continued to train for the inevitable war with Japan. ENTERPRISE (CV-6), LEXINGTON (CV-2), and SARATOGA (CV-3) were assigned to Pearl Harbor, Hawaii, which offered improved positioning to counter Japanese moves in the Pacific. (The US Pacific Fleet headquarters was transferred from San Diego, California to Pearl Harbor in May of 1940.) The Pacific Fleet carrier air groups were provided with the latest fighting aircraft. The F4F and Brewster F2A Buffalo provided fighter protection, the Douglas **SBD Dauntless** was assigned to scouting and dive-bombing duties, and the TBD performed torpedo and level bombing missions.

The brightly colored aircraft from the late 1930s and early 1940s gave way to an overall Nonspecular (Flat) Light Gray (FS36493) scheme authorized for carrier aircraft on 30 December 1940. On 13 October 1941, this scheme was amended to have Nonspecular Blue-Gray (FS35189) upper surfaces, while undersurfaces remained Light Gray. The Blue-Gray finish offered improved camouflage against observation from above the aircraft. The undersurfaces of folding outer wing sections were also painted Blue-Gray to camouflage these surfaces on the flight deck. Squadron insignia were removed and unit identity was confined to fuselage codes painted on each aircraft.

At 0755 hours on Sunday, 7 December 1941, 183 aircraft from six Japanese carriers operating north of the Hawaiian Islands attacked US Army and Navy installations on the Island of Oahu. A second wave of

The Curtiss SBC Helldiver assigned to the Commander of the ENTERPRISE (CV-6) Air Group is started on the deck of YORKTOWN (CV-5) during carrier qualifications in early 1941. The aircraft's cowl striping and tail were True Blue (FS15102) – the color assigned to ENTERPRISE's aircraft before 1941. The carrier's Scouting Squadron Six (VS-6) flew the SBC until April of 1941. (Via US Navy)

170 Japanese aircraft attacked at 0840 hours. Their goal was to strike a devastating blow to the battleships and carriers that were stationed at Pearl Harbor. Fortunately for the US, all three carriers were at sea and escaped any damage. The eight battleships were not so fortunate and all were either damaged to some extent or destroyed. The US lost many aircraft on the ground, but the biggest loss was in personnel with over 2400 American soldiers, sailors, and civilians killed and over 1100 wounded. The greatest loss of life occurred on the battleship **ARIZONA** (BB-39), where over half of the fatalities occurred. The US lost 169 aircraft while the Japanese lost only 29.

In the next few days, Japanese naval, ground, and air forces attacked US forces in the Philippines, Guam, and Wake Island. By the end of 1941, the US Navy had suffered bitter humiliation and defeat at Japanese hands.

Douglas SBD-3 Dauntlesses from Bombing Squadron Three (VB-3) and Douglas TBD-1 Devastators from Torpedo Squadron Three (VT-3) warm up their engines prior to taking off from the YORKTOWN in early 1941. The aircraft were painted in the overall Nonspecular Light Gray (FS36493) 'peacetime' scheme authorized on 30 December 1940. Fuselage codes were white and no unit insignia appeared on the aircraft. National insignia were painted on the aft fuselage, upper port wing, and lower starboard wing. The propeller spinners are missing from some of these SBD-3s. (National Archives)

A Douglas TBD-1 is in the 'groove' and under power to recover safely aboard ENTERPRISE in July of 1941. The Landing Signal Officer (LSO) will soon give the 'cut' signal to the pilot. The pilot then cuts his engine, turning him into a glider pilot for recovery onto the flight deck. The LSO's job was not an easy chore, since it required the skill of a pilot and the nerve of a daredevil to stand so close to the landing aircraft. Brightly colored paddles in the LSO's hands allow him to clearly guide the pilot through the final approach. The raised canvas panel beside the LSO was a windshield used when the LSO was not guiding aircraft aboard the carrier. (National Archives)

Douglas TBD-1s from Torpedo Squadron Three (VT-3) line up for launch from USS SARATOGA (CV-3) in mid-1941. The TBD Devastator was the most modern torpedo bomber and the first all-metal aircraft accepted by the US Navy. Another Douglas product, an SBD-3 Dauntless, follows the Devastators along the flight deck. Shuffleboard courts were painted on the flight deck for crew recreation purposes. (United Technologies Archives)

A Grumman F4F-3 Wildcat (3-F-9, BuNo 3982) from Fighting Squadron Three (VF-3) is brought up on an elevator aboard SARATOGA in October of 1941. Ensign Gayle Hermann was the pilot assigned to this F4F-3; however, the plane captain is seated in the cockpit during this procedure. The Wildcat is camouflaged in the overall Light Gray scheme. In October of 1941, this scheme was altered to include Blue-Gray (FS35109) upper surfaces. Other Wildcats are tied down on the after flight deck. The F4F-3 entered US Navy service with VF-4 and VF-7 in December of 1940. (National Archives)

8

A flight deck aircraft director signals a Grumman F4F-3 from Fighting Squadron Three (VF-3), believed to be piloted by Lt. John S. Thach, down SARATOGA's wood deck in October of 1941. Lt. Thach was credited with developing the 'Thach weave,' an aerial maneuver designed to overcome the superiority of the Japanese A6M Zero fighter in a dogfight. (National Archives)

Under the close supervision of a Chief Petty Officer, a VF-3 F4F-3 Wildcat undergoes fuselage and port wing repairs on SARATOGA's hangar deck in October of 1941. The 'Felix the Cat' squadron emblem appeared on the fuselage below the windshield. Spare SBDs from Scouting Squadron Two (VS-2) and TBD-1s from Torpedo Squadron Three (VT-3) were suspended from the overhead structure to make room on the hangar deck. (National Archives)

Mechanics repair the port wing tip of a Grumman F4F-3, under a Navy Chief's watchful eye. One mechanic was drilling out some rivets, while a colleague sitting on the hangar deck dimpled the head of a rivet. It was not uncommon for carrier-based aircraft to be damaged during normal handling in the ship's close confines. (Real War Photos)

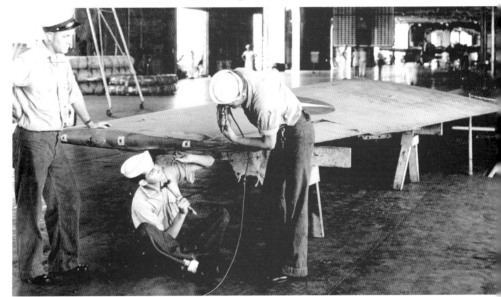

US Navy Carrier-Based Squadron Designators, 1941-1945

VB	Bombing Squadron
VC	Composite Squadron
VF	Fighting Squadron
VFB	Fighter-Bomber Squadron
VGS	Escort Scouting Squadron
VS	Scouting Squadron
VT	Torpedo Squadron
(N)	Night

The starboard wing oil cooler inlet of a VF-3 F4F-3 (3-F-2, BuNo 3973) is inspected on SARATOGA's hangar deck in October of 1941. Spare propellers were hung from overhead racks. Some propeller tips were striped (from outermost) Insignia Red (FS11136), Chrome Yellow (FS13538), and Insignia Blue (FS15042). This was the pre-war US Navy propeller tip coloring. Other propellers were tipped Orange Yellow (FS33538), which became the US Navy's standard propeller warning color from 28 August 1942. Propeller blades were flat black, while hubs and cuffs were natural metal. (Real War Photos)

9

Ensign Arthur J. Brassfield (left) oversees maintenance of one of Fighting Squadron Forty-Two's (VF-42) F4F-3A Wildcats aboard YORKTOWN at Casco Bay, Maine on 13 November 1941. The mechanic has placed a file in his back pocket, which posed a risk of injury to his back in the event of a fall. The SBD-3 parked off the Wildcat's port wing was armed with a submarine depth bomb under the fuselage. YORKTOWN operated with the Atlantic Fleet until transferred to the Pacific shortly after the Pearl Harbor attack on 7 December 1941. (National Archives)

Lt. (later Capt) David McCampbell, Landing Signal Officer (LSO), brings on aircraft aboard WASP (CV-7) in late 1941. Standing behind McCampbell was the Assistant Landing Signal Officer, Ensign George E. 'Doc' Savage. In the lower center catwalk are Len Ford (enlisted rating) and Lt. Hawley Russell. Lt. McCampbell and Ens. Savage each wore a yellow pullover vest to increase their visibility to the pilots. McCampbell went on to become the highest scoring Navy ace of the Pacific War, with 34 Japanese aircraft kills. (National Archives)

A Vought SB2U-3 Vindicator (42-S-17) assigned to Scouting Squadron Forty Two (VS-42) circles USS RANGER (CV-4) while awaiting the launch of its escorting F4F-3 Wildcats from Fighting Squadron Forty Two (VF-42). Seven Wildcats awaited the signal from 'Fly One' (First Flight Officer) to launch from the deck. RANGER was the first US aircraft carrier designed from the keel-up and was com-missioned on 4 July 1934. Her slow speed (29 knots) and lack of armor protection caused the carrier to be used in the Atlantic for much of World War Two. She was equipped with six side-mounted funnels – three per side – which swung outboard during flight operations. (Elsilrac)

A Curtiss SOC-3A Seagull (201-S-2) from Scouting Squadron 201 (VS-201) is tied down on the deck of the escort carrier LONG ISLAND (CVE-1) in December of 1941. The carrier operated in the Atlantic. The SOC is armed with a centerline-mounted 325 pound Mk 17 submarine depth bomb. This variant of the Seagull – an aircraft better known for operating on floats from cruisers – was equipped with an arresting hook immediately in front of the tail wheel. The fuselage code was black. (National Archives)

SB2U Vindicators from VS-41 and VS-42 and a F4F-3 Wildcat from VF-41 prepare to launch from RANGER on a scouting mission in late 1941. All aircraft are camouflaged in the Nonspecular (Flat) Blue-Gray (FS35189) over Nonspecular Light Gray (FS36493) scheme. The nearest SB2U (42-S-13) was fitted with a 325 pound (147.4 KG) Mk 17 depth bomb on the centerline bomb cradle. The Vindicator never flew into combat from a carrier; however, shore-based Marine SB2Us operated during the Battle of Midway in June of 1942. (Via US Navy)

1942 – Taking the fight to the Japanese and Germans

US Navy carrier forces began taking the fight to the Japanese on 1 February 1942 – 56 days after the attack on Pearl Harbor – with raids on the Marshall and Gilbert Islands. The attacks were designed to keep the Japanese from mounting an invasion of any more islands around the area of Australia and to let the Japanese know that the US Navy still had a presence in the Pacific.

The US Navy received its first air ace of World War Two on 20 February 1942. Lt. (jg) Edward 'Butch' O'Hare of Fighting Squadron Three (VF-3) from USS LEXINGTON (CV-2) intercepted a formation of 17 Mitsubishi **G4M** bombers (Allied codename **Betty**) sent to attack his carrier. Flying a Grumman F4F-3A Wildcat, O'Hare shot down five of the bombers and had a probable victory on a sixth. He was duly awarded the Medal of Honor for his heroism. O'Hare was reported missing in action after a mission in 1943.

On 18 April 1942, the US first struck the Japanese home islands in a joint Army-Navy effort. Lt. Col. Jimmy Doolittle (US Army Air Forces; USAAF) led 16 North American **B-25B Mitchell** bombers from the rain slicked deck of the carrier HORNET (CV-8) to raid Tokyo and other Japanese cities. The attack caused little physical damage to the targets, but they were of immense positive psychological value to the Americans. The result of the raid began to convince the Japanese of the folly of their attacks on Pearl Harbor and the rest of the Allies' Pacific Sphere of Influence. When President Franklin Roosevelt was asked where the bombers took off from, he replied "Shangri-La," a mythical island from the novel 'Lost Horizon.' To commemorate the raid, the US Navy named a carrier the **SHANGRI-LA** (CV-38) in 1944.

A historic naval battle occurred in the Coral Sea on 7-8 May, when US forces confronted a Japanese amphibious landing force headed for Port Moresby in New Guinea. The carriers YORKTOWN and LEXINGTON launched their air groups; the Japanese carriers followed suit. The ensuing attacks marked the first time a major engagement was made by opposing fleets at sea without the naval forces engaging with their respective ships. All contact with the enemy fleet was made by air. During the ensuing battle, the LEXINGTON was abandoned and sunk following repeated aerial torpedo and bomb hits. The YORKTOWN was damaged, requiring quick repairs at Pearl Harbor. The Japanese lost their light carrier **SHOHO**, while the carrier **SHOKAKU** was damaged. Deprived of air cover, the Japanese invasion force turned away from Port Moresby. The Battle of the Coral Sea was the TBD Devastators' finest hour.

The Japanese decided to attack Midway Island in early June, although they were unaware that their secret code had been broken and the US was aware of their plans. Task Force 17, with the now repaired YORKTOWN, and Task Force 16 with ENTERPRISE (CV-6) and HORNET launched attacks on the Japanese carrier forces on the morning of 4 June. Japanese carrier aircraft were attacking Midway at the time and were unprepared to make adequate defense of their forces. Forty one TBDs from Torpedo Squadrons Five, Six, and Eight (VT-5, 6, and 8) attacked the Japanese carriers with their torpedoes, but failed to score a single hit. The Mitsubishi A6M **Zero** (Allied codename **Zeke**) Combat Air Patrol and anti-aircraft (AA) fire from the ships downed 37 of the 41 Devastators, including all 15 TBDs of the HORNET's VT-8. While the Zeros were finishing off the torpedo aircraft, SBD Dauntless dive-bombers attacked the Japanese carriers. When the Battle of Midway ended on 6 June, the Japanese had lost four of their carriers – **AKAGI**, **KAGA**, **SORYU**, and **HIRYU** – and the US lost the YORKTOWN. This decisive battle effectively ended Japanese offensive operations in the Pacific and they were on the defensive for the balance of the war. The Battle of Midway saw the debut of the Grumman **TBF-1 Avenger** torpedo bomber, operated by a shore-based element from Torpedo Squadron Eight (VT-8). The detachment fared no better than their squadron mates from the HORNET, losing five of the six aircraft sent from Midway to attack the Japanese carriers on 4 June. This was an inauspicious start to a career that soon saw the TBF replace the TBD as the premier torpedo bomber for US Navy carrier operations.

On 7 August 1942, the US invaded the island of Guadalcanal in the Solomons (Operation WATCHTOWER). This began a campaign that took six months to complete. A Japanese submarine's torpedo damaged SARATOGA (CV-3) on 31 August and another submarine sank WASP (CV-7) while it escorted a convoy to Guadalcanal on 15 September. The HORNET was sunk one month later off the Island of Santa Cruz by concentrated Japanese aerial attacks. This left only the ENTERPRISE to fight the Japanese, prompting the crew of the carrier to erect a banner in the hanger deck proclaiming "Enterprise vs. Japan."

While the fighting in the Pacific raged on, a different type of battle was being waged in the Atlantic, a battle with the German U-Boats (from *unterseeboot*; submarine). The U-Boats were taking a terrific toll on the Allied convoys carrying supplies to England and Russia and a solution had to be quickly found. It came in the form of the escort carriers (CVEs) with their destroyer escorts (DEs). The solution was to scout off the carriers using the F4F fighters and TBF bombers. Once the surfaced subs were located either with the new Air-to-Surface Type B (ASB) radar, High Frequency/Direction Finding (HF/DF) equipment, or by visual observations, the force would attack. Increased availability of escort carriers resulted in more U-Boats being sunk. These Hunter-Killer Groups would almost completely rid the Atlantic of the U-Boat scourge by war's end. Lighter-than-air blimps (non-rigid airships) eventually joined these forces in providing air cover for Allied convoys.

The last major carrier campaign for the US Navy in 1942 was the November invasion of French North Africa. Operation TORCH involved the fleet carrier RANGER (CV-4) and the new escort carriers **SANGAMON** (CVE-26), **SUWANNEE** (CVE-27), **CHENANGO** (CVE-28), and **SANTEE** (CVE-29). F4F Wildcats and USAAF Curtiss **P-40F Warhawks** flying off the carriers provided air cover, with the P-40s landing at newly-captured airfields in French Morocco and Algeria. Carrier-based SBDs flew scouting and dive-bombing missions.

An SOC-3A from VS-201 is tied down to the snow-covered aft flight deck of LONG ISLAND (CVE-1) in early 1942. The escort carrier operated in the Atlantic with the battleship WASHINGTON (BB-56). The pierced metal stanchions in front of the Seagull served as windbreaks for the fierce North Atlantic winds. (National Archives)

A VT-6 TBD-1 makes an approach to ENTERPRISE (CV-6) following a scouting flight in early 1942. The LSO is guiding the Devastator pilot on his final approach. The assistant LSO standing behind the LSO would have called to his colleague, "Gear down, flaps down, hook down, all down!" The LSO's paddles are brightly colored for maximum visibility. The TBD-1 is still armed with a 500 pound (226.8 KG) bomb on the centerline bomb rack. (National Archives)

A TBD-1 (2-T-6) assigned to VT-6 crosses the aft flight deck ramp. The pilot had just received the 'cut' signal from the LSO to land aboard ENTERPRISE on 1 February 1942. This aircraft returned with empty bomb racks after attacking targets on Wake Island. 'Fiddle bars' raise the arresting cables above the flight deck, which enabled the aircraft's tail hook to engage the cable. (National Archives)

A VT-6 TBD-1 prepares to snag the number six 'wire' (cable) on ENTERPRISE following a bombing mission in early 1942.The LSO and Assistant LSO peek around the side of the wind screen to observe the landing. Soon after the aircraft stopped, a deck crewman known as the 'hook man' would approach the tail. He then disengaged the tail hook from the arresting cable, which allowed the aircraft to taxi forward and clear the aft flight deck for the next aircraft to land.

VT-6 TBD-1s and VF-6 F4F-3s are spotted on the flight deck of ENTERPRISE prior to raiding Wake Island on 24 February 1942. Japanese forces captured Wake from its US Marine defenders in December of 1941. The size and placement of the national insignia on the wings and fuselage varied among aircraft. Rudders of US Navy aircraft were painted with red and white stripes from 23 December 1941. (National Archives)

A TBD-1 Devastator assigned to VT-6 is framed by the landing gear and undersurface of another Devastator from this unit aboard ENTERPRISE. The near aircraft was armed with a 500 pound bomb on its centerline rack. Dark blue canvas covers were placed over the canopy and rudder stripes to reduce their observation by Japanese reconnaissance aircraft. The Devastators attacked Japanese-held Wake Island on 24 February 1942. (National Archives)

An aircraft machinist begins cranking the inertial starter of a VT-6 TBD-1 Devastator (White 13) aboard ENTERPRISE on 17 April 1942. He stood on a fold-down work platform on the forward fuselage, immediately aft of the engine cowling. The Devastator was launched on a scouting flight in the northwest Pacific while escorting HORNET (CV-8), which was carrying Lt Col 'Jimmy' Doolittle's B-25s towards their launch point for Japan. The TBD-1 was armed with six 100 pound (45.4 KG) bombs under the wings – three bombs under each wing. The bombardier has already occupied his position behind the pilot. (National Archives)

Lt. Cdr. Lex A. Black makes the 2000th landing aboard LONG ISLAND (CVE-1) in April of 1942. Black, Commander of Escort Scouting Squadron One (VGS-1), flew an SOC-3A Seagull (1-GS-12). LONG ISLAND was the US Navy's first escort carrier and was commissioned on 2 June 1941. She served as a training carrier and aircraft transport in the Atlantic throughout World War Two and was decommissioned in March of 1946. (National Archives)

Armorers test fire the six wing-mounted .50 caliber (12.7MM) machine guns of a VF-6 F4F-4 Wildcat (6F9) aboard ENTERPRISE in April of 1942. The black fuselage aircraft designator lacked the usual separating dashes. A dark blue canvas cover was placed over the striped rudder of this Wildcat. This cover camouflaged the rudder while the aircraft was parked on the flight deck. (National Archives)

The destroyer DUNLAP (DD-384) cuts close across the stern of ENTERPRISE while operating near Hawaii on 8 April 1942. The Task Force charged with conducting the Doolittle Raid on Japan – centered on the carriers HORNET and ENTERPRISE – departed from Pearl Harbor that day. Deck crews spotted SBD Dauntlesses of VB-6 on ENTERPRISE's aft flight deck. (National Archives)

A VF-8 F4F-3 Wildcat (F-26) shares flight deck space with North American B-25B Mitchell bombers aboard HORNET. False tail turrets – using painted broom handles and painted slots in the clear tail cone – were intended to mislead Japanese pilots attacking the B-25. Steel cables secured the aircraft to metal hooks placed throughout the flight deck. HORNET was unable to fly her own aircraft with Doolittle's B-25s aboard and relied on ENTERPRISE for air cover until the B-25s were launched. (National Archives)

US Army Air Forces B-25B Mitchells cover HORNET's flight deck while she steams into the wind on 18 April 1942. Soon after this maneuver, the Doolittle Raiders were launched for Japan. The Mitchells were stripped of their ventral turrets to save weight for the additional gasoline required to extend their range. The B-25s were each armed with three 500 pound bombs and an incendiary cluster. (National Archives)

The B-25 Mitchell piloted by Lt Col James H. 'Jimmy' Doolittle launches from HORNET's deck on the morning of 18 April 1942, bound for Japan. The takeoff was accomplished in less than 300 feet (91.4 M) of deck space and into a head wind of approximately 40 knots (46.1 MPH/74.1 KMH). The 15 other B-25s were successfully launched within one hour of Doolittle's departure. The Mitchells were launched soon after HORNET was spotted by a Japanese picket vessel 600 miles (965.6 KM) east of Japan – approximately 200 miles (321.9 KM) east of the intended launch point. The Doolittle Raid caused little physical damage to targets in Japan, but was of immense psychological value to the Americans at home and in uniform. (National Archives)

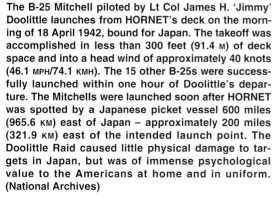

15

VB-5 SBD-3 Dauntless dive-bombers are spotted forward on YORKTOWN's flight deck during operations in the Coral Sea in April of 1942. VB-5 painted individual aircraft numbers on the engine cowling, while VS-5 – also equipped with SBDs – painted their aircraft numbers on the wing leading edges. The near aircraft's number 3 was originally white, but was later overpainted black. (National Archives)

A Supermarine Spitfire Vc (C-4, BP865) takes off from WASP (CV-7) while in the western Mediterranean Sea in May of 1942. The US carrier delivered 47 Royal Air Force (RAF) Spitfires to Malta in April of 1942 (Operation CALENDAR), followed by 47 more fighters in May (Operation BOWERY). These aircraft helped bolster British defenses on Malta against constant German and Italian raids. The Spitfires were equipped with a 90 gallon (340.7 L) long-range slipper tank under the fuselage for the 660 mile (1062.1 KM) flight to Malta. The aircraft were believed to be camouflaged in Midstone (FS30266) and Dark Earth (FS30118) upper surfaces and Azure Blue (FS35231) undersurfaces. (National Archives)

A VF-6 F4F-4 Wildcat (Black 7) launches from ENTERPRISE during operations in the Coral Sea on 18 May 1942. After escorting HORNET on the Doolittle Raid mission, ENTERPRISE was deployed south to reinforce LEXINGTON and YORKTOWN; however, ENTERPRISE arrived too late to aid in the Battle of the Coral Sea. The Wildcat received the new national insignia, which was adopted on 6 May 1942. This removed the red disc from the center of the star and the red and white rudder stripes. A black 7 was painted on the fuselage beneath the canopy. (National Archives)

A VT-6 TBD-1 Devastator is brought up on the aft elevator of ENTERPRISE on 4 June 1942, prior to the Battle of Midway. The aircraft was armed with a 2216 pound (1005.2 KG) Mk 13 torpedo semi-recessed under the fuselage. The Devastator's outer wings folded hydraulically. Folded wings allowed more aircraft to be embarked aboard carriers. VT-6 launched 14 TBDs at the Japanese carriers at Midway; only four Devastators survived this attack. (National Archives)

Eleven of VT-6's 14 TBD-1s are spotted on ENTERPRISE's after flight deck on the morning of 4 June 1942. The three remaining Devastators were soon brought to this position prior to launching the Squadron's aircraft. Lt. Cdr. Eugene Lindsey led VT-6 in its unsuccessful attack on the Japanese carriers at Midway. Only four of the 41 TBDs launched from ENTERPRISE, HORNET, and YORKTOWN survived the attacks and none scored a torpedo hit. (National Archives)

An SBD-3 Dauntless (B15, BuNo 4542) of ENTERPRISE's VB-6 is parked aboard YORKTOWN after landing at approximately 1140 hrs on 4 June 1942. This aircraft was damaged by Japanese anti-aircraft fire while attacking the aircraft carrier KAGA during the Battle of Midway. The Dauntless lacked enough fuel to reach ENTERPRISE and recovered aboard YORKTOWN. This SBD was lost when YORKTOWN was sunk early on 5 June. Dauntlesses were responsible for successfully attacking all four Japanese carriers deployed to Midway. The two white parallel stripes on the vertical stabilizer enabled the LSO to determine the aircraft's angle of attack during approach and recovery. (National Archives)

17

Crewmen repair bomb damage to the flight deck of YORKTOWN soon after a Japanese 250 KG (551.1 pound) bomb hit the carrier during the Battle of Midway on 4 June 1942. The hole was soon repaired using timber and steel plating, which allowed flight deck operations to resume. Several water-cooled .50 caliber anti-aircraft machine guns were fitted along YORKTOWN's deck-edge catwalks. This weapon was soon replaced by the 20MM Oerlikon cannon, which was a more effective light anti-aircraft gun. (National Archives)

A Brewster F2A-3 Buffalo from Marine Fighter Squadron 211 (VMF-211) lands in the catwalk of the escort carrier LONG ISLAND in July of 1942. The carrier was on a brief cruise off Palmyra Island in the central Pacific. Flight deck crewmen rushed to aid the pilot and secured the aircraft with lines to prevent it from going overboard. The Buffalo never saw combat from a carrier deck. Shore-based Marine F2As were decimated by more agile Japanese A6M Zeros during the Battle of Midway. (National Archives)

Brewster F2A-3 Buffalo

Several senior officers gather on the port bridge of WASP while the carrier operated off Guadalcanal in the Solomon Islands on 7 August 1942. A water-cooled .30 caliber (7.62MM) machine gun was mounted to the bridge bulwark for anti-aircraft protection. The SBDs parked on WASP's flight deck had different variations of the national insignia. Two of the Dauntlesses had the white star shade painted to reduce visibility from observation from above. SBD number 4's fuselage side star was greatly reduced in size. (National Archives)

(Above) F4F-4 Wildcats assigned to VF-71 and SBD Dauntlesses from VS-71 and VS-72 are spotted on WASP's flight deck on 9 August 1942. The carrier was operating off Guadalcanal early in the US campaign against the Japanese-held Solomon Islands. Most deck crewmembers were equipped with a personal floatation device and M1 'steel pot' army-style helmets. The helmets protected the heads from flying debris, including shrapnel. WASP was escorting resupply convoys when a Japanese submarine sank her off Guadalcanal on 15 September 1942. (Real War Photos)

(Below) Deck crewmen lift an overturned F4F-4 Wildcat, which had just struck the crash barrier while recovering aboard WASP in August of 1942. The steel cable barrier protected aircraft and personnel from aircraft unable to be arrested by the cables. The pilot was freed from the cockpit after the aircraft was sufficiently lifted. Most crewmen carried a gas mask pouch, since it was believed the Japanese would use poison gas bombs during attacks. The masks were deemed unnecessary and were discarded after late 1942. (Real War Photos)

A J2F-1 Duck recovers aboard USS CHARGER (CVE-30) in mid-1942. The tailhook extended from the Duck's aft fuselage, behind the rear of the center float. This amphibian aircraft was assigned to the ship's utility squadron, which flew training and 'hack' (personnel transport) missions for the carriers. Most US aircraft carriers were assigned a utility squadron during World War Two. CHARGER was converted from an incomplete cargo ship acquired by the US Navy and commissioned on 3 March 1942. She never saw combat; instead, she was deployed to the Atlantic to train US and British carrier pilots. (Real War Photos)

(Left) An aircraft handling crane hoists an F4F-4 Wildcat from the aircraft transport KITTY HAWK (AVP-1) to the deck of the escort carrier LONG ISLAND in the fall of 1942. The white star in the wing national insignia was covered with tape to reduce recognition. What is believed to be an early style 42 gallon (159 L) auxiliary fuel tank has been fitted to the Wildcat's lower fuselage. This tank was soon replaced on Wildcats by two 58 gallon (219.6 L) drop tanks under the wings. (Real War Photos)

(Below) Curtiss P-40F Warhawk fighters crowd the hangar deck of USS CHENANGO (CVE-28) in October of 1942. The escort carrier delivered the USAAF fighters to the coast of French North Africa for the Allied invasion (Operation TORCH). The P-40s were brought up to the flight deck and launched to help provide air cover for the invasion fleet. The Warhawks were camouflaged in Olive Drab (FS34087) and Sand (FS30279), with Neutral Gray (FS36173) undersurfaces. Fuselage national insignia had not yet received the yellow outer ring specified for Allied aircraft involved in Operation TORCH. (National Archives)

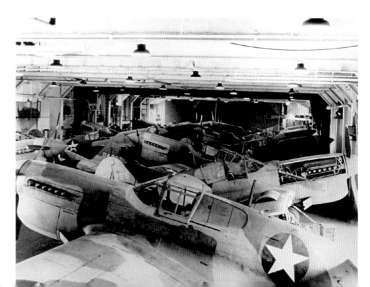

Ordnancemen load .30 caliber armor piercing ammunition onto an SBD-3 Dauntless (Black 2) aboard USS SANTEE (CVE-29) in October of 1942. The ammunition belts were fed into two ammunition boxes mounted to the aft cockpit bulkhead. These boxes held ammunition for the two rear cockpit machine guns fired by the radio operator/rear gunner. The aircraft from Escort Scouting Squadron Twenty Nine (VGS-29) was prepared for a scouting mission prior to helping cover the British and American invasion of French North Africa the following month. A 250 pound (113.4 KG) bomb was mounted under each wing. (Real War Photos)

A Mark 13 aerial torpedo is loaded into a VGS-29 TBF-1 Avenger (Black 10) aboard SANTEE on 29 October 1942. The escort carrier was assigned to the invasion force for Operation TORCH. The Avenger's pilot stood near the folded starboard wing while he observed the ordnancemen maneuvering the torpedo into the bomb bay. (Real War Photos)

21

Ordnance crews test fire the six .50 caliber Browning machine guns of F4F-4 Wildcats aboard USS RANGER (CV-4) in November of 1942. The fighters were assigned to VF-9 and VF-41 aboard the carrier, which was approaching the coast of French North Africa. Wildcats from RANGER provided air cover for the Allied invasion force during Operation TORCH. The Orange Yellow (FS33538) ring applied around the fuselage national insignia aided recognition of friendly aircraft for Allied anti-aircraft gunners. British aircraft deployed for TORCH also used US national insignias with Orange Yellow borders on the fuselage. (National Archives)

A VF-9 F4F-4 (Black 2) makes a successful 'trap' (arrested landing) aboard RANGER on 8 November 1942 – the opening day of Operation TORCH. The cockpit canopy was left open on carrier launches and recoveries to assist the aircrew in evacuating the aircraft in the event of a crash. The Wildcat is camouflaged in the standard US Navy scheme of Blue-Gray upper surfaces and Light Gray undersurfaces. Two more F4Fs fly off RANGER's starboard side to enter the landing pattern for recovery aboard the carrier. RANGER and four escort carriers – SANGAMON (CVE-26), SUWANNEE (CVE-27), CHENANGO (CVE-28), and SANTEE (CVE-29) – provided carrier-based air power for US forces assaulting French Morocco and Algeria. (Real War Photos)

Grumman F4F-4 Wildcat

Elizabeth, a USAAF Piper L-4A-PI Cub (42-36389), is prepared for take off aboard RANGER on 8 November 1942. The observation aircraft's engine was started by manually turning the propeller, since the L-4 was not equipped with an electric starter. The propeller tips, cowl, and the national insignia outer ring were Orange Yellow. The rest of the wood propeller was Flat Black (FS37038). RANGER launched three L-4s to provide aerial reconnaissance and forward air control for the attacking Allied Fleet. (National Archives)

A VF-41 F4F-4 Wildcat launches from RANGER to attack Axis targets in French North Africa early in Operation TORCH. Two USAAF L-4 Cubs circled the carrier before flying towards the beachhead. Fighters from the five US carriers deployed for TORCH clashed with pro-Axis Vichy French aircraft over North Africa. Wildcat pilots claimed 26 Vichy French aircraft destroyed and another five aircraft probably destroyed, for a loss of nine F4Fs to French fighters. (National Archives)

Deck handlers park a VGS-29 SBD-3 Dauntless (Black 10) on SANTEE's forward flight deck on 27 December 1942. Aircraft 11, parked on the port bow, had its black fuselage side number aft of the national insignia, with the other three Dauntlesses have their numbers forward of the insignia. SBDs 10 and 14 have flat Insignia Red (FS31136) propeller spinners. The SBD's lack of wing folding reduced its deployment aboard escort carriers after Operation TORCH, in favor of TBF/TBM Avengers. (Real War Photos)

1943 – The Tide Turns in the Atlantic and Pacific

By 1943, US naval forces had been at war for a little over one year and they had the Japanese on the run in the Pacific. In the Mediterranean Theatre, the Germans faced defeat in North Africa. The US and her Allies made plans to attack Italy, beginning with the invasion of Sicily on 10 July. The main US naval effort – including the carrier forces – would remain in the Pacific.

The **USS ESSEX** (CV-9), lead ship for a class of 13 fleet carriers, was commissioned on 31 December 1942. She began working up for duty in the Pacific at the beginning of 1943. In May, ESSEX arrived in the southwest Pacific to relieve ENTERPRISE (CV-6, nicknamed the 'Big E'), which had been the only US fleet carrier in the area since October of 1942. The US would commission and place six more ESSEX class fleet carriers into service during 1943. Nine **INDEPENDENCE** class light carriers (CVLs) and 19 **CASABLANCA** class escort carriers (CVEs) also entered US Navy service the same year.

In the Atlantic, aircraft from the escort carrier **BOGUE** (CVE-9) sank the German submarine **U-569** in the Mid-Atlantic on 22 May. This marked the first submarine 'kill' by an escort carrier Hunter-Killer Group. Grumman F4F Wildcat fighters and TBF Avenger torpedo bombers assigned to Composite Squadron Nine (VC-9) located U-569 on the surface approximately ten miles (16.1 KM) astern of the carrier. The TBFs dropped depth bombs, which straddled the U-Boat and caused extensive damage. The submarine's crew scuttled their boat to prevent its capture by the Americans. US escort carriers helped provide continuous air cover for Allied convoys. This was one step that enabled the Allies to gain the upper hand in the Battle of the Atlantic from May of 1943.

Three new aircraft types began to grace US carrier flight decks during 1943. The Vought **F4U Corsair** was finally accepted on the deck following carrier qualification aboard **USS BUNKER HILL** (CV-17) in July of 1943. This fighter – nicknamed 'whistling death' by the Japanese and the 'bend-wing bird' by those privileged to fly the Corsair – earned a reputation for toughness unequaled by only a few other US Navy aircraft. In August, the Grumman **F6F-3 Hellcat** was used in combat flying off ESSEX and **YORKTOWN** (CV-10)[1] for the first time, during a raid on Marcus Island. The Hellcat gave US Navy pilots the added speed and firepower necessary to defeat the Japanese Zero. This year also saw the successful introduction of the Curtiss **SB2C-1 Helldiver** dive-bomber, which also flew off BUNKER HILL to attack targets in Rabaul, New Britain. The Helldiver earned many nicknames, but perhaps the most enduring was 'big assed bird.' The Hellcat, Corsair, and Helldiver would eventually form the backbone of the US carrier air groups in attacks on the Japanese in the Pacific.

A new three-tone aircraft camouflage system was authorized for use from 5 January 1943, replacing the Blue Gray over Light Gray finish employed since October of 1941. The new scheme consisted of Nonspecular (flat) Sea Blue (FS35045) upper surfaces blended into Intermediate Blue (FS35164) sides over Nonspecular White (FS37875) undersurfaces. Wing and horizontal stabilizer upper surfaces were Semi-Gloss Sea Blue (FS25045) with Nonspecular Sea Blue leading edges. This scheme was seen on carrier aircraft until the end of the war in the Pacific. Atlantic Fleet carrier based aircraft had Dark Gull Gray (FS36231) upper surfaces with Nonspecular White sides and undersurfaces.

[1]This ESSEX class carrier was named for the previous YORKTOWN (CV-5), sunk at the Battle of Midway in June of 1942.

A North American SNJ-3C trainer suffered a landing gear collapse upon landing aboard the training carrier CHARGER (CVE-30) in 1943. The starboard gear strut broke and the cowl and wings were also damaged as the aircraft hit the steel cable crash barrier. The SNJ-3C was fitted with a tailhook taken from Grumman F3F fighters. The SNJ, the Navy version of the USAAF's AT-6 Texan, was used to train naval aviators the skill of making 'controlled crash' landings. In many instances, the landings culminated in a damaged aircraft. (Elsilrac)

An SOC Seagull assigned to VGS-12 makes an arrested landing aboard USS COPAHEE (CVE-12) in early 1943. VGS squadrons used Seagulls for training and 'hack' roles from their ships. The SOC was also designed to operate on floats in the scouring role from cruisers and battleships. COPAHEE was the third of 11 BOGUE class escort carriers commissioned between September of 1942 and April of 1943. (Real War Photos)

This Brewster F2A-1 Buffalo (3-F-1, BuNo 1396) was assigned to the Commander of Fighting Squadron Three (VF-3) – the famous 'Felix the Cat' squadron – aboard USS SARATOGA (CV-3) in 1940.

The 'Neutrality Star' national insignia was painted on the forward fuselage of this Grumman F4F-3 Wildcat (41-F-7). The fighter was assigned to VF-41 on RANGER (CV-4), which operated in the Atlantic during 1940.

The red tail of this Northrop BT-1 (5-B-14, BuNo 0614) identifies it as serving with Bombing Squadron Five (VB-5) aboard YORKTOWN (CV-5) in 1940.

Scouting Squadron Six (VS-6) operated this Curtiss SBC-3 (6-S-5, BuNo 0569) aboard ENTERPRISE (CV-6) in 1940. The Helldiver was flown in both scouting and dive-bombing roles.

During Fleet Problem XXI in 1940, this Douglas TBD-1 (BuNo 0339) from Torpedo Squadron Three (VT-3) on SARATOGA was painted in the experimental Barclay camouflage scheme. This scheme used geometric patterns of a bluish green applied over Aluminum lacquer.

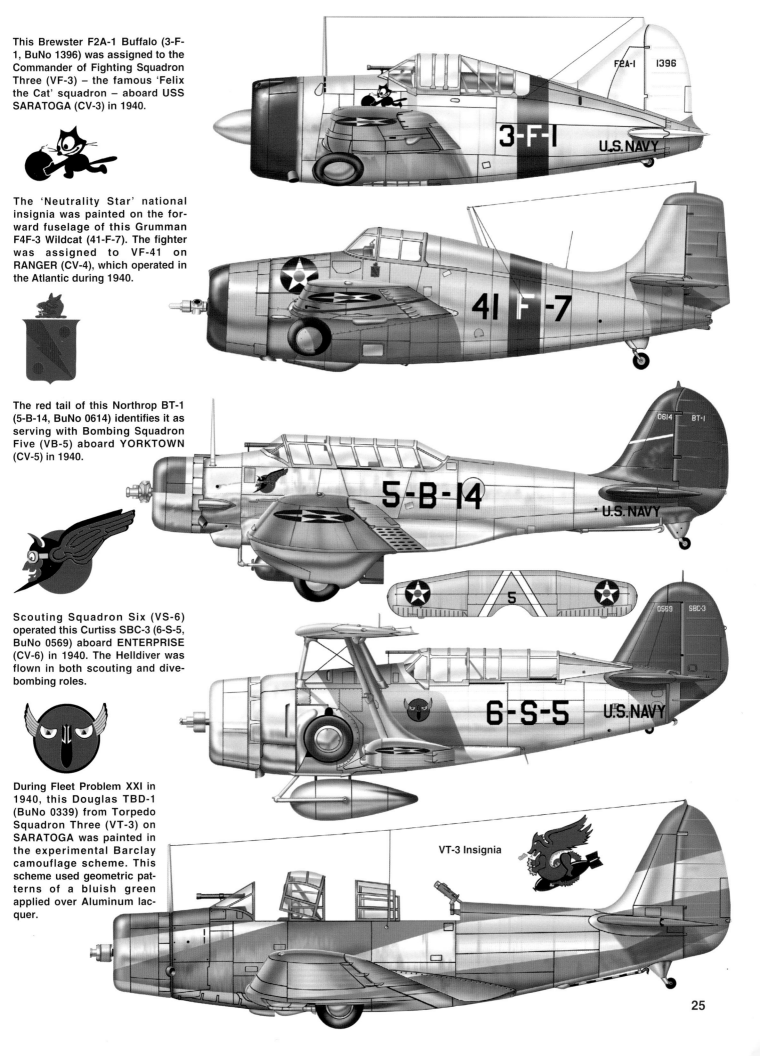

25

A Grumman F6F-3 Hellcat (33) assigned to VF-9 is prepared for launch from USS ESSEX (CV-9) in May of 1943. Deck crewmen unfolded the Hellcat's wings and locked them into position for flight. This aircraft was fitted with streamlined gun covers for the two inboard .50 caliber (12.7MM) wing-mounted machine guns. These covers were fitted to the first 900 F6Fs built, but were deleted from later Hellcats. The fighter was painted Blue-Gray (FS35189) over Light Gray (FS36493). (Via Jim Sullivan)

A VF-2 F6F-3 Hellcat taxis forward with its wings folded during training exercises aboard ENTERPRISE (CV-6) on 2 July 1943. A deck crewman near the Hellcat's starboard side used hand signals to direct the pilot toward his parking spot on the flight deck. Another F6F flies over ENTERPRISE with its landing gear and flaps lowered and its tail hook extended. This fighter had just received a wave off from the Landing Signal Officer (LSO), due to a fouled deck. He re-entered the landing pattern to make another recovery attempt. (National Archives)

Grumman F6F-3 Hellcat

BETS, a TBM-1 (Eastern Aircraft-built TBF-1) is raised on the aircraft-handling elevator of USS COPAHEE on 11 September 1943. The Avenger was assigned to the ship's Escort Carrier Air Group 50 (CVEG-50). Nose art or names were unusual on carrier aircraft and usually required the squadron commander's permission for it to be applied. White sidebars and red trim were added to the US national insignia on 28 June 1943. The upper starboard wing displayed evidence of fresh paint applied over the national insignia. The TBM-1 was fitted with Yagi Air to Surface Type B (ASB) radar antennas on the wing undersurfaces. (Real War Photos)

Ordnancemen service 500 pound (226.8 KG) and 1000 pound (453.6 KG) bombs amid VF-5 F6F-3 Hellcat fighters parked on the hangar deck of the ESSEX class carrier YORKTOWN (CV-10) in late 1943. The 00 ('double nuts') painted on the near F6F's folded starboard wing indicated the aircraft was assigned to the Commander of Air Group (CAG). These Hellcats were finished in the three-tone camouflage scheme – Nonspecular Sea Blue (FS35045), Intermediate Blue (FS35164), and Nonspecular White (FS37875) – authorized on 5 January 1943. Other crewmen watched the latest movie projected on a white screen suspended from the hangar's overhead structure. (National Archives)

A VF-2 F6F-3 (30) crashed into the port side 20MM anti-aircraft gun gallery on ENTERPRISE on 10 November 1943. The impact ruptured the centerline 150 gallon (567.8 L) fuel tank, which resulted in the Hellcat catching fire. The ships' Catapult Officer, Lt. Walter L. Chewing Jr., US Naval Reserve (USNR), climbed up the F6F's side to assist the pilot in evacuating the aircraft. The pilot, Ensign Byron M. Johnson, escaped this accident without significant injury. ENTERPRISE was en route to support the US invasion of the Gilbert Islands when this incident occurred. (National Archives)

Eastern Aircraft TBM-1 Avenger

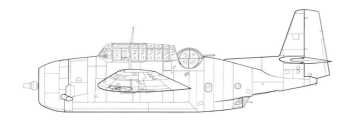

Ordnancemen prepare to load a 250 pound (113.4 KG) general purpose bomb and Mk 41 depth charges onto a VT-10 TBM-1 Avenger aboard YORKTOWN on 20 November 1943. Aircraft machinists worked on the upper forward fuselage while the aircraft was 'bombed up' for a mission against Japanese defenses on the Marshall Islands. The Avenger's bomb bay held either a torpedo or up to 2000 pounds (907.2 KG) of ordnance. (Real War Photos)

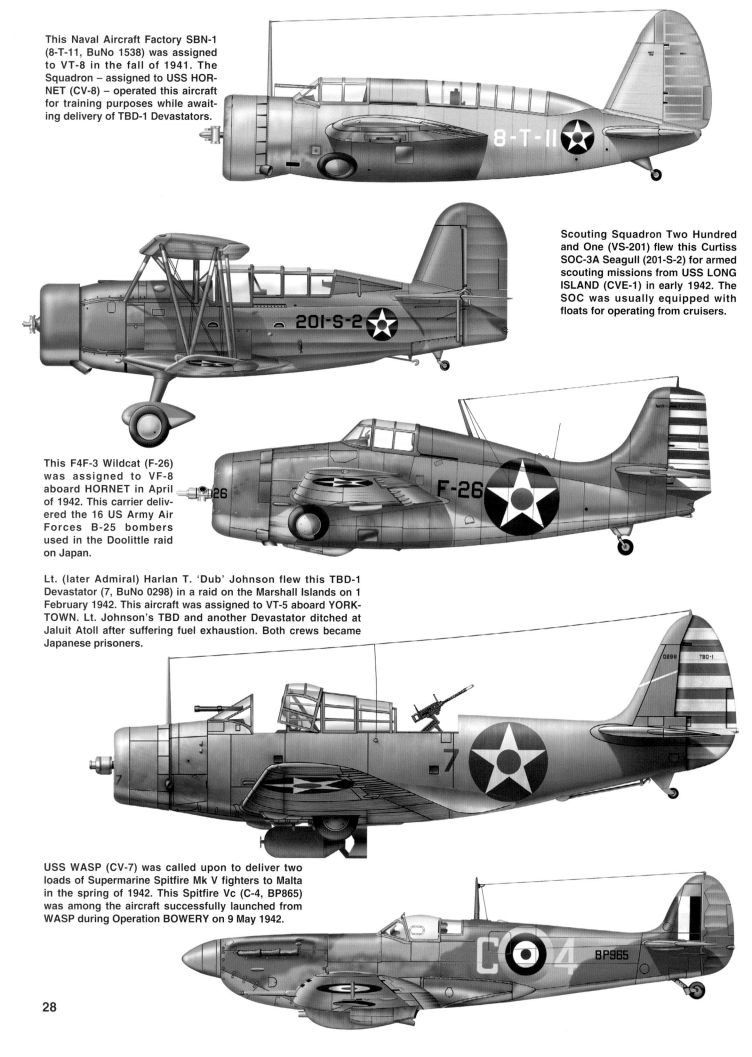

This Naval Aircraft Factory SBN-1 (8-T-11, BuNo 1538) was assigned to VT-8 in the fall of 1941. The Squadron – assigned to USS HORNET (CV-8) – operated this aircraft for training purposes while awaiting delivery of TBD-1 Devastators.

Scouting Squadron Two Hundred and One (VS-201) flew this Curtiss SOC-3A Seagull (201-S-2) for armed scouting missions from USS LONG ISLAND (CVE-1) in early 1942. The SOC was usually equipped with floats for operating from cruisers.

This F4F-3 Wildcat (F-26) was assigned to VF-8 aboard HORNET in April of 1942. This carrier delivered the 16 US Army Air Forces B-25 bombers used in the Doolittle raid on Japan.

Lt. (later Admiral) Harlan T. 'Dub' Johnson flew this TBD-1 Devastator (7, BuNo 0298) in a raid on the Marshall Islands on 1 February 1942. This aircraft was assigned to VT-5 aboard YORKTOWN. Lt. Johnson's TBD and another Devastator ditched at Jaluit Atoll after suffering fuel exhaustion. Both crews became Japanese prisoners.

USS WASP (CV-7) was called upon to deliver two loads of Supermarine Spitfire Mk V fighters to Malta in the spring of 1942. This Spitfire Vc (C-4, BP865) was among the aircraft successfully launched from WASP during Operation BOWERY on 9 May 1942.

VB-6 flew this SBD-3 (B4) from ENTER-
PRISE in February of 1942. The
Dauntless was armed with a 1000
pound (453.6 KG) bomb for a raid on
Wake Island.

Aircraft T-5 (BuNo 0308) was one of 15 TBD-1s
launched from HORNET on 4 June 1942. All of
VT-8's Devastators were lost in their unsuccessful attacks on the Japanese carriers that
morning, during the Battle of Midway.

Ensign Leif Larsen of
VS-5 (formerly VB-5)
was assigned this
SBD-3 Dauntless (17)
on YORKTOWN during
the Battle of Midway
on 4 June 1942. The
carrier's SBDs sank
the Japanese carriers
SORYU and HIRYU
during the clash.

VS-41 flew this Vought SB2U-3 Vindicator (41-S-8) from RANGER
in early 1942. The Squadron's aircraft conducted armed scouting
missions in the Atlantic; however, the Vindicators did not see
action in this theater of war.

VF-6 aboard ENTERPRISE had
a tombstone painted on the vertical stabilizers of their F4F-3s.
The 41 'meatballs' on the tombstone represented Japanese
aircraft downed by the
Squadron. Machinist Mate
Donald F. Runyon flew aircraft
13 (BuNo 5193) during the
Guadalcanal campaign in
August of 1942. He scored eight
'kills' with this Wildcat.

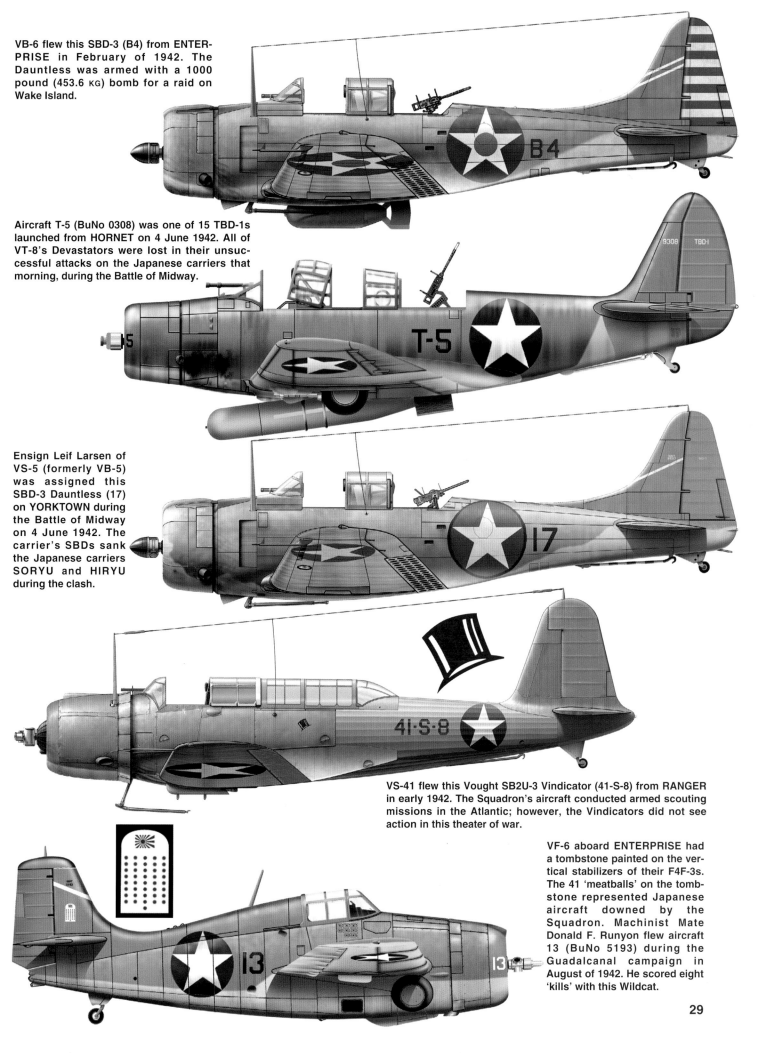

29

Condensation rings swirl from the propeller tips of an F6F-3 Hellcat awaiting the take-off flag aboard YORKTOWN (CV-10) on 20 November 1943. This effect resulted from the humid air through which the propeller blades rotated. The F6F was assigned to VF-5, which combined with the carrier's other squadrons in hitting Japanese targets in the Marshall Islands. This raid covered the US invasion of the Gilbert Islands, located southeast of the Marshalls. VF-5 was previously assigned to the old carrier YORKTOWN (CV-5), which was sunk during the Battle of Midway in June of 1942. (National Archives)

The pilot of a VF-25 F6F-3 Hellcat (BuNo 66101) runs onto the starboard wing to escape his burning aircraft in November of 1943. The aircraft caught fire after recovering aboard the light carrier COWPENS (CVL-25). The deck fire crew moved forward to apply fire suppressant foam to the 150 gallon centerline fuel tank, which had ruptured upon landing. Aircraft damaged in this manner were usually jettisoned from the carrier into the water. (National Archives)

Two Curtiss P-40K Warhawks from the USAAF's 15th Fighter Group (FG) are spotted on the flight deck of the escort carrier BRETON (CVE-23) on 10 December 1943. Aircraft number 215 was assigned to the 78th Fighter Squadron (FS) with white numerals and two Orange Yellow cowl bands. P-40 number 158 was assigned to the 47th FS, whose squadron insignia appeared on the cowling above the engine exhaust stacks. The name HATTIE HAWGMEAT was painted under the exhausts and two blue bands were applied to the cowling. An ordnanceman walking between the two P-40s pulled a 354 pound (160.6 KG) Mark 54 depth bomb on a dolly. The vertical tail in the foreground belonged to an Eastern Aircraft FM-2 Wildcat assigned to BRETON's air group. (Real War Photos)

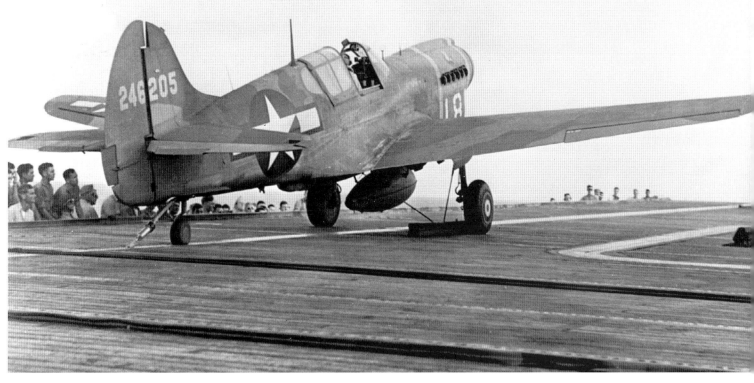

(Above) A P-40K Warhawk (18/42-46205) of the 6th Night Fighter Squadron, 15th FG prepares to launch from BRETON on 10 December 1943. Steel cables secured the wing undersurfaces and tail to the ship's catapult. The Warhawk was sent to reinforce US air defenses at Canton Island in the Phoenix Island Group. The P-40 was camouflaged with Sand (FS30279) and Olive Drab (FS34087) upper surfaces, while undersurfaces were Neutral Gray (FS36173). A 150 gallon fuel tank was mounted on the centerline. (Real War Photos)

(Below) The pilot of this TBM-1 is about to have a bad day while his Avenger crashes into the port side catwalk aboard USS CABOT (CVL-28) on 14 December 1943. The extended tail hook is about to catch the barrel of a 20mm Oerlikon anti-aircraft cannon. The deck crew near the parked aircraft on the forward flight deck began to take cover after realizing the Avenger was making an uninvited arrival to their area. The wing national insignia included the blue trim around the center circle and side bars. This replaced the red insignia trim from 31 July 1943. (Real War Photos)

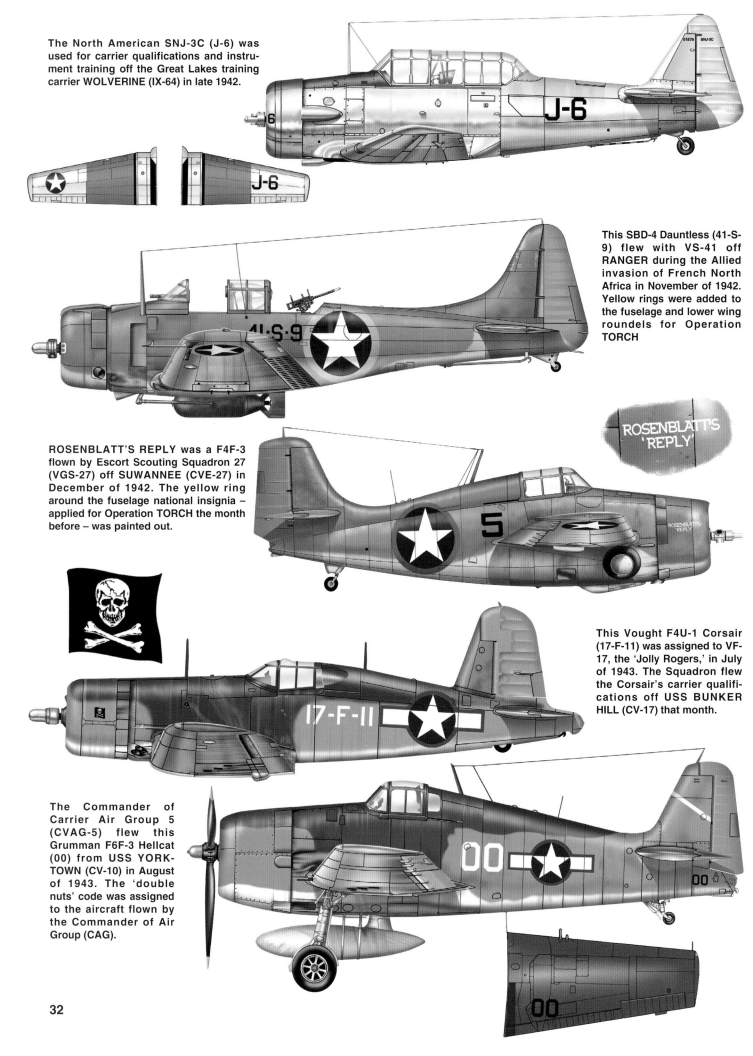

The North American SNJ-3C (J-6) was used for carrier qualifications and instrument training off the Great Lakes training carrier WOLVERINE (IX-64) in late 1942.

This SBD-4 Dauntless (41-S-9) flew with VS-41 off RANGER during the Allied invasion of French North Africa in November of 1942. Yellow rings were added to the fuselage and lower wing roundels for Operation TORCH

ROSENBLATT'S REPLY was a F4F-3 flown by Escort Scouting Squadron 27 (VGS-27) off SUWANNEE (CVE-27) in December of 1942. The yellow ring around the fuselage national insignia – applied for Operation TORCH the month before – was painted out.

This Vought F4U-1 Corsair (17-F-11) was assigned to VF-17, the 'Jolly Rogers,' in July of 1943. The Squadron flew the Corsair's carrier qualifications off USS BUNKER HILL (CV-17) that month.

The Commander of Carrier Air Group 5 (CVAG-5) flew this Grumman F6F-3 Hellcat (00) from USS YORK-TOWN (CV-10) in August of 1943. The 'double nuts' code was assigned to the aircraft flown by the Commander of Air Group (CAG).

BETS (18) was an Eastern Aircraft TBM-1C from
VT-21. This Avenger flew off the escort carrier
COPAHEE (CVE-12) in September of 1943.

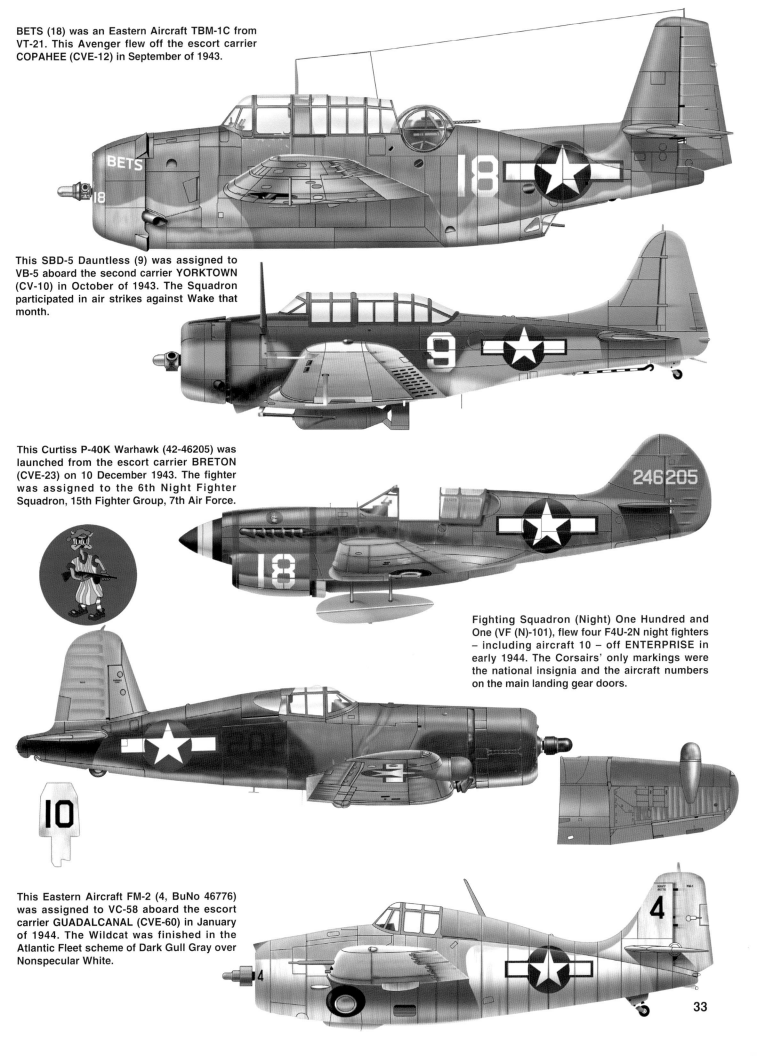

This SBD-5 Dauntless (9) was assigned to
VB-5 aboard the second carrier YORKTOWN
(CV-10) in October of 1943. The Squadron
participated in air strikes against Wake that
month.

This Curtiss P-40K Warhawk (42-46205) was
launched from the escort carrier BRETON
(CVE-23) on 10 December 1943. The fighter
was assigned to the 6th Night Fighter
Squadron, 15th Fighter Group, 7th Air Force.

Fighting Squadron (Night) One Hundred and
One (VF (N)-101), flew four F4U-2N night fighters
– including aircraft 10 – off ENTERPRISE in
early 1944. The Corsairs' only markings were
the national insignia and the aircraft numbers
on the main landing gear doors.

This Eastern Aircraft FM-2 (4, BuNo 46776)
was assigned to VC-58 aboard the escort
carrier GUADALCANAL (CVE-60) in January
of 1944. The Wildcat was finished in the
Atlantic Fleet scheme of Dark Gull Gray over
Nonspecular White.

1944 – The Year of Triumphs, Defeats, and the *Kamikaze*

The year 1944 began with innovations in attacking surfaced German U-Boats in the Atlantic. On 11 January, two TBF-1Cs from Composite Squadron 58 (VC-58) off **USS BLOCK ISLAND** (CVE-21) located **U-758** on the surface and attacked it with air-to-surface rockets. Two to four rockets hit the submarine; however, it was able to reach a friendly port. BLOCK ISLAND became the only US carrier lost in the Atlantic when she was sunk by U-549 while operating a Hunter-Killer air group off the Canary Islands on 29 May. This U-Boat was sunk a few minutes later by the destroyer escort **EUGENE E. ELMORE** (DE-686).

On 29 January, the US began invading the Marshall Islands in the Pacific, supported by six fleet and six light carriers. The carrier air groups completely eliminated the Japanese air forces allowing complete mastery of the air. On the morning of 29 January, eight escort carriers arrived with their air groups to provide anti-submarine patrols and to attack Japanese shipping. The invasion was completed and all US objectives were accomplished by 22 February. It was during the Marshall Island attacks that the US Navy's first night bombing attacks took place. The raids were carried out by 12 radar equipped TBF-1C Avengers assigned to Torpedo Squadron Ten (VT-10) aboard ENTERPRISE (CV-6).

The camouflage color scheme of carrier based fighter aircraft was changed from the three-tone scheme adopted in 1943 to an overall Glossy Sea Blue (FS15042) finish on 13 March. This was extended to all other carrier based aircraft by an order issued on 26 June and effective on 7 October. The implementation of the Glossy Sea Blue scheme was slow to catch on and the three-tone scheme could still be seen on fighters in late 1945.

Carrier-based aircraft first dropped aerial mines in late March, when TBF-1s of Torpedo Squadrons Two, Eight, and Sixteen (VT-2, 8, and 16) mined Palau Harbor in the Western Carolines. These attacks coincided with strikes in the Western Carolines that denied Japanese use of the harbor. US naval forces destroyed 157 Japanese aircraft and sank 28 Japanese ships displacing a total of 108,000 tons.

The U-Boat war in the Atlantic heated up on 4 June, when a Hunter-Killer group captured the German **U-505** off the Azores. Determined attacks by aircraft from Composite Squadron Eight (VC-8) aboard the escort carrier **GUADALCANAL** (CVE-60) and five destroyer escorts forced the submarine to surface. The U-505 is now displayed at the Museum of Science and Industry in Chicago, Illinois, USA.

Two days later – on 6 June 1944, D-Day – combined Allied forces landed at Normandy, France (Operation OVERLORD). Air attacks were launched from the Allies' unsinkable aircraft carrier – England. US Naval Aviators flew Royal Air Force **Spitfires** on gunfire spotting missions over the Normandy beaches on D-Day. It would take almost one more year before Germany's final defeat became a reality.

In the Pacific, the US began invading the Marianas on 15 June. The assault began with air attacks on the Japanese-held islands from the seven fleet carriers and eight light carriers of Task Force 58. The islands of Saipan, Guam, Bonin, and Volcano were attacked and eventually overtaken by amphibious forces. The Japanese responded with attacks that proved fatal for their attacking bombers and fighters. During the Battle of the Philippine Sea (19-20 June), US aircraft and anti-aircraft guns downed 402 Japanese aircraft. The US lost only 23 aircraft to enemy fire, prompting them to call this one-sided action the 'Great Marianas Turkey Shoot.'

The last major battle of 1944 occurred on and around the Philippine Island of Leyte from 10 October to 30 November. The Japanese defended the island with great ferocity, despite being outnumbered in ships and aircraft. The Battle for Leyte Gulf resulted in the loss of the light carrier **PRINCETON** (CVL-23) to Japanese aircraft on 24 October. The escort carrier **GAMBIER BAY** (CVE-73) was sunk by gunfire from the Japanese super battleship **YAMATO** during the battle off of Samar on 25 October.

The Japanese response to the US Navy at Leyte Gulf was to employ *kamikaze* ('divine wind') suicide aircraft for the first time. These suicide attacks sank the escort carrier **ST. LO** (CVE-63) and damaged the **SANGAMON** (CVE-26), **SUWANNEE** (CVE-27), **SANTEE** (CVE-29), **WHITE PLAINS** (CVE-66), and **KITKUN BAY** (CVE-71). Although the Japanese had taken a terrible toll of American lives, they lost 26 major warships – including four carriers – totaling over 300,000 tons and over 770 aircraft to American forces.

The year 1944 ended with the Germans facing eminent defeat and the Japanese continuing their tenacious defense of the Pacific islands. More major battles loomed on the horizon for the US carrier forces, mainly in the Pacific.

Crewmen prepare to load a 2000 pound (907.2 KG) general-purpose bomb in the weapons bay of a VT-18 TBM-1 Avenger (85) aboard USS INTREPID (CV-11) on 27 January 1944. The carrier was en route to support the invasions of Roi and Namur Islands on Kwajalein Atoll in the Marshalls. The bomb was inscribed by Torpedoman 3rd Class R.A. Franco and addressed to 'HON. HIROHITO, IMPERIAL PALACE, TOKYO.' The TBM was fitted with exhaust flame dampers for night operations. (National Archives)

Crewmen spot F6F-3 Hellcats of VF-10 on the flight deck of ENTERPRISE (CV-6) in February of 1944. A Jeep towed one of the Hellcats (71) into position on the forward flight deck. Jeeps were modified for flight deck operations through the installation of battery cables, which were used to help start the aircraft. These and other US Navy general service vehicles were painted gray (approximately FS36187). A Vought F4U-2 Corsair of Fighting Squadron (Night) One Hundred and One (VF(N)-101) was spotted near the aft end of the carrier's 'island' super-structure. (Floating Drydock)

Fleet and Light Carriers in the Pacific, 1944

SARATOGA	CV-3
ENTERPRISE	CV-6
ESSEX	CV-9
YORKTOWN	CV-10
INTREPID	CV-11
HORNET	CV-12
FRANKLIN	CV-13
TICONDEROGA	CV-14
LEXINGTON	CV-16
BUNKER HILL	CV-17
WASP	CV-18
HANCOCK	CV-19
INDEPENDENCE	CVL-22
PRINCETON	CVL-23
BELLEAU WOOD	CVL-24
COWPENS	CVL-25
MONTEREY	CVL-26
LANGLEY	CVL-27
CABOT	CVL-28
BATAAN	CVL-29
SAN JACINTO	CVL-30

F6F-3 assigned to VF-10 'Grim Reapers' recover aboard ENTERPRISE after attacking the Japanese base at Truk in the Caroline Islands on 17 February 1944. Flight deck crewmen folded the Hellcat's wings and guided the aircraft forward to the parking area on the forward flight deck. VF-10 was assigned to Carrier Air Group Ten (CVG-10) aboard ENTERPRISE for operations against the Carolines. The Hellcats were camouflaged in the three-tone scheme of Nonspecular Sea Blue (FS35045) upper surfaces, Intermediate Blue (FS35164) sides, and Nonspecular White (FS37875) undersurfaces. (National Archives)

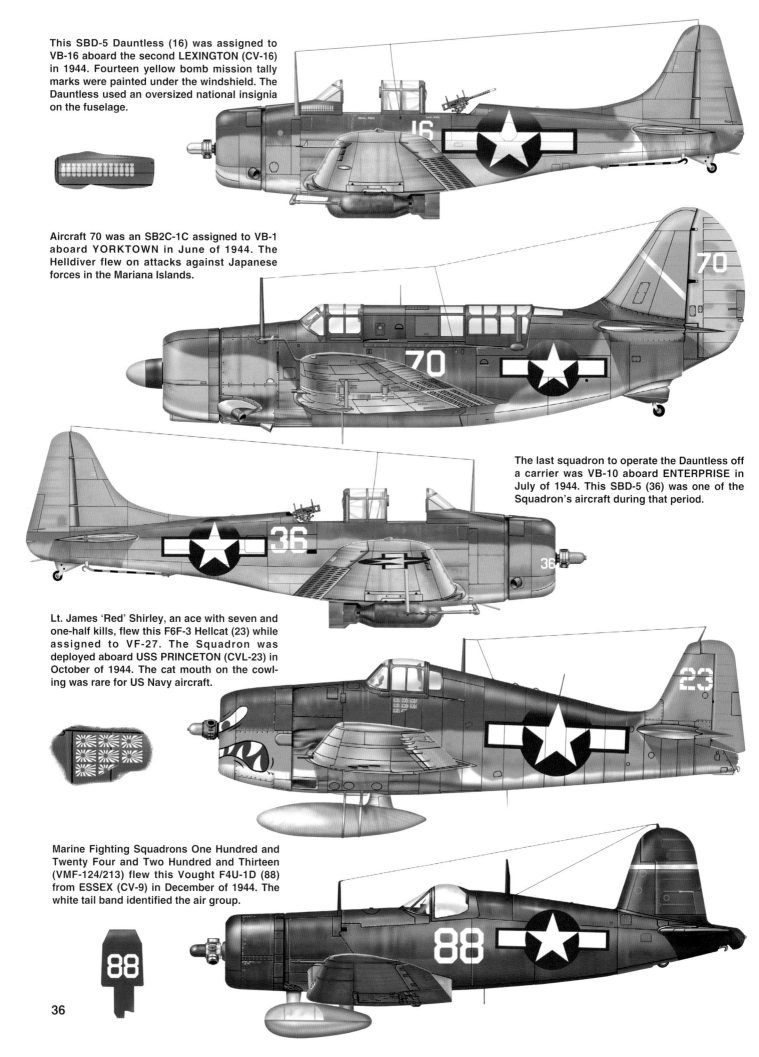

This SBD-5 Dauntless (16) was assigned to VB-16 aboard the second LEXINGTON (CV-16) in 1944. Fourteen yellow bomb mission tally marks were painted under the windshield. The Dauntless used an oversized national insignia on the fuselage.

Aircraft 70 was an SB2C-1C assigned to VB-1 aboard YORKTOWN in June of 1944. The Helldiver flew on attacks against Japanese forces in the Mariana Islands.

The last squadron to operate the Dauntless off a carrier was VB-10 aboard ENTERPRISE in July of 1944. This SBD-5 (36) was one of the Squadron's aircraft during that period.

Lt. James 'Red' Shirley, an ace with seven and one-half kills, flew this F6F-3 Hellcat (23) while assigned to VF-27. The Squadron was deployed aboard USS PRINCETON (CVL-23) in October of 1944. The cat mouth on the cowling was rare for US Navy aircraft.

Marine Fighting Squadrons One Hundred and Twenty Four and Two Hundred and Thirteen (VMF-124/213) flew this Vought F4U-1D (88) from ESSEX (CV-9) in December of 1944. The white tail band identified the air group.

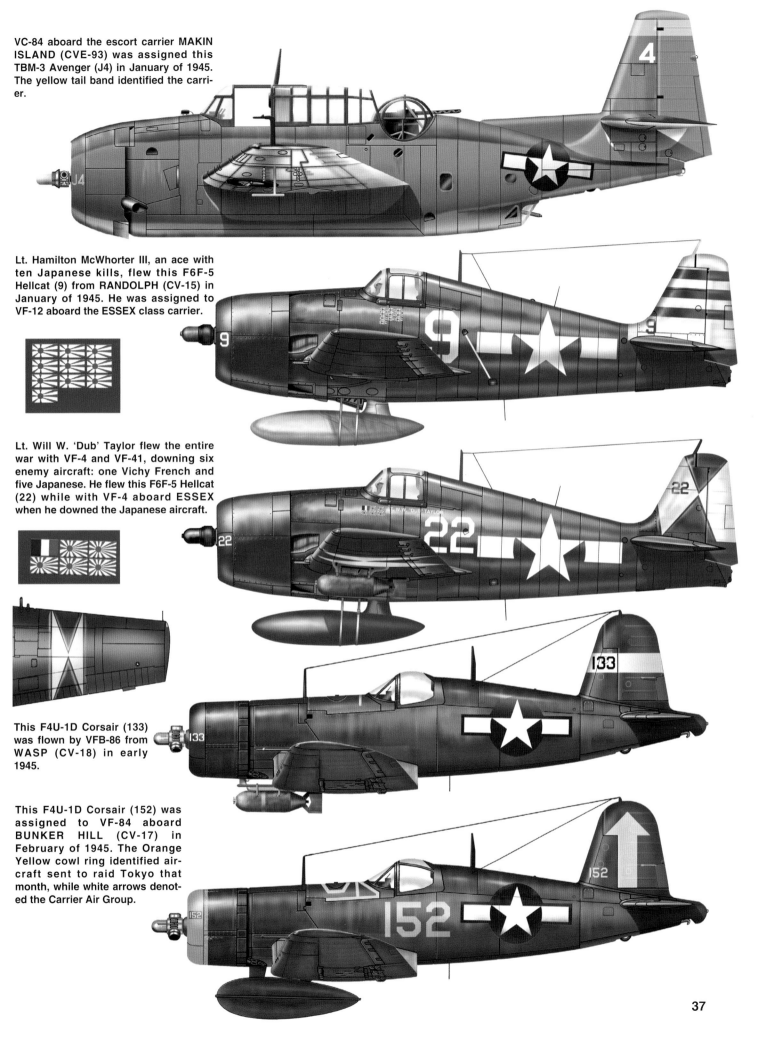

VC-84 aboard the escort carrier MAKIN ISLAND (CVE-93) was assigned this TBM-3 Avenger (J4) in January of 1945. The yellow tail band identified the carrier.

Lt. Hamilton McWhorter III, an ace with ten Japanese kills, flew this F6F-5 Hellcat (9) from RANDOLPH (CV-15) in January of 1945. He was assigned to VF-12 aboard the ESSEX class carrier.

Lt. Will W. 'Dub' Taylor flew the entire war with VF-4 and VF-41, downing six enemy aircraft: one Vichy French and five Japanese. He flew this F6F-5 Hellcat (22) while with VF-4 aboard ESSEX when he downed the Japanese aircraft.

This F4U-1D Corsair (133) was flown by VFB-86 from WASP (CV-18) in early 1945.

This F4U-1D Corsair (152) was assigned to VF-84 aboard BUNKER HILL (CV-17) in February of 1945. The Orange Yellow cowl ring identified aircraft sent to raid Tokyo that month, while white arrows denoted the Carrier Air Group.

A VF-2 F6F-3 (21) is launched from the hangar deck of the second carrier HORNET (CV-12) on 12 February 1944. The first five ESSEX class carriers each had a hangar deck catapult; only HORNET retained hers until the end of World War Two. The Hellcat faced a cross wind of approximately 35 knots (40.3 MPH/64.9 KMH) on launch, which required a considerable amount of control correction. (National Archives)

A VC-12 FM-2 Wildcat (20) is launched from the escort carrier CORE (CVE-13) in the Atlantic in April of 1944. The fighter was camouflaged in the Dark Gull Gray (FS36231) over Nonspecular White (FS37875) scheme designed for operations over the Atlantic Ocean. CORE and her Task Group was credited with sinking five German U-Boats (submarines). (National Archives)

VC-36 F4F-4 Wildcats are prepared for catapult launching from USS MISSION BAY (CVE-59), during Atlantic operations on 7 June 1944. The landing gear struts were painted the same Nonspecular White as the aircraft undersurfaces. This color helped the Landing Signal Officer (LSO) acquire the F4F at night. (Real War Photos)

A VF-28 F6F-3 Hellcat (3) clears the catapult of USS MONTEREY (CVL-26) during operations near the Mariana Islands in June of 1944. The catapult crew retrieved the steel catapult bridle left by the F6F. This bridle connected the catapult to a pair of hardpoints on the aircraft's undersurface. Another crewman carried a bridle for use by the next aircraft. A plexiglas wind screen was fitted to the open bridge area. (National Archives)

A flight deck officer prepares to signal take-off to the pilot of a VT-28 TBM-1 (15) on MONTEREY in June of 1944. The Avenger was launched to attack Japanese targets on Tinian Island in the Marianas. Fake machine guns ports were painted on the leading edge of the lead TBM-1. These ports were intended to confuse Japanese pilots into thinking this Avenger was an F6F Hellcat fighter. The TBM-1 was actually armed with one .50 caliber machine gun in each wing. (National Archives)

The launch officer on USS ESSEX (CV-9) gives the 'Go' signal to a VT-4 TBM-1C in the summer of 1944. The Avenger was part of a strike force sent to attack a Japanese convoy northwest of Saipan in the Mariana Islands. The TBM was armed with eight 5 inch (12.7 CM) High Velocity Aerial Rockets (HVARs), mounted on zero length launch rails on the wing undersurfaces. Yagi antennas for Air-to-Surface Type B (ASB) radar were mounted under each wing's outboard section. (Real War Photos)

A TBM-1C (81/BuNo 48102) assigned to VT-2 recovers aboard HORNET on 13 June 1944. The Avenger's starboard outer wing was damaged by Japanese anti-aircraft fire. The VT-2 insignia appeared on the forward fuselage, ahead of eleven white bomb mission symbols. The symbols were arranged in two rows of five and a solitary bomb symbol starting a third row. This Avenger was also equipped with an AN-A6 gun camera on the upper forward fuselage, while another camera was mounted on the ventral gunner's 0.50 caliber machine gun. The white circle below the numeral 81 on the tail indicated HORNET's air group. (Via Jim Sullivan)

A Republic P-47D Thunderbolt (29), *Dee-Icer*, is hooked to the catapult of MANILA BAY (CVE-61) prior to launch in June of 1944. The aircraft was assigned to the USAAF's 78th Fighter Squadron (FS), 315th Fighter Group. The Thunderbolt had Olive Drab upper surfaces and Neutral Gray undersurfaces. The front cowling and tail band were white, while the Squadron's 'Bar Flies' insignia was placed on the cowl side. A mouth with teeth was painted on the 75 gallon (283.9 L) centerline fuel tank. MANILA BAY ferried the 78th FS's P-47s to the Mariana Islands, where they bolstered US air defenses. (Real War Photos)

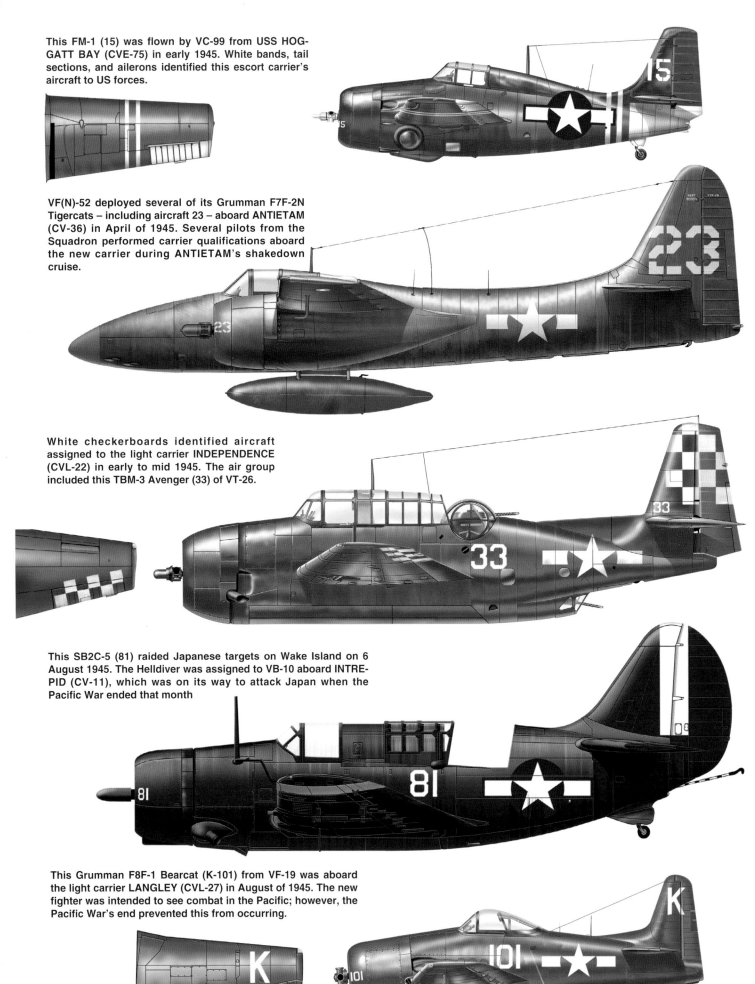

This FM-1 (15) was flown by VC-99 from USS HOG-GATT BAY (CVE-75) in early 1945. White bands, tail sections, and ailerons identified this escort carrier's aircraft to US forces.

VF(N)-52 deployed several of its Grumman F7F-2N Tigercats – including aircraft 23 – aboard ANTIETAM (CV-36) in April of 1945. Several pilots from the Squadron performed carrier qualifications aboard the new carrier during ANTIETAM's shakedown cruise.

White checkerboards identified aircraft assigned to the light carrier INDEPENDENCE (CVL-22) in early to mid 1945. The air group included this TBM-3 Avenger (33) of VT-26.

This SB2C-5 (81) raided Japanese targets on Wake Island on 6 August 1945. The Helldiver was assigned to VB-10 aboard INTRE-PID (CV-11), which was on its way to attack Japan when the Pacific War ended that month

This Grumman F8F-1 Bearcat (K-101) from VF-19 was aboard the light carrier LANGLEY (CVL-27) in August of 1945. The new fighter was intended to see combat in the Pacific; however, the Pacific War's end prevented this from occurring.

A VF-9 F6F-3 tipped onto its nose during recovery aboard ESSEX in mid-1944. The Hellcat broke its arresting hook upon landing and engaged the crash barrier extended across the flight deck. A white recognition band on the vertical tail appeared on aircraft assigned to ESSEX from mid-1943 until early 1945. The Hellcat was finished in the three-tone scheme: Nonspecular Sea Blue, Intermediate Blue, and Nonspecular White. This aircraft appeared to have been damaged by either anti-aircraft fire or the crash on the port wing leading edge and flap.(Floating Drydock)

A VT-2 TBM-1 Avenger (93) rests against the island superstructure of HORNET following a crash landing in mid-1944. The impact sheared off the starboard outer wing and damaged the port wing tip. The white circle emblem for HORNET's air group was painted below the aircraft number on the vertical stabilizer. Deck crewmen later salvaged useable parts from the Avenger before the wreck was hoisted by an aircraft recovery crane and dumped overboard. HORNET's scoreboard was placed just above the TBM's aft fuselage. This scoreboard recorded aircraft and ships destroyed or damaged by the carrier's aircraft during the war. (Floating Drydock)

Catapult crewmen hook up a VC-93 FM-2 Wildcat (10) onto the catapult shuttle aboard USS MANANIKAU (CVE-101) on 27 July 1944. The shuttle moved within the catapult track on the flight deck. A bridle connected this shuttle to hard points on the aircraft's undersurface, which allowed the aircraft to be catapulted from the deck. The

Wildcat's pilot had received the 'Hold' signal from the flight deck officer while his aircraft was prepared for launch. The catapult officer bent over under the starboard wing to monitor his crew's application of the catapult bridle. (Real War Photos)

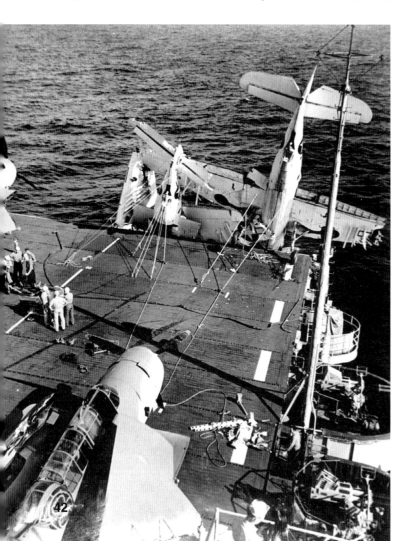

(Left) A VC-79 TBM missed the arresting cables while recovering aboard the escort carrier BOGUE (CVE-9) in the Atlantic in July of 1944. The Avenger jumped the crash barrier and crashed into other TBMs spotted on the forward flight deck. One Avenger was sent overboard while three others were damaged in the accident. (Real War Photos)

(Below) The US Navy blimp (non-rigid airship) K-85 receives assistance upon landing on an escort carrier in the Atlantic in mid-1944. The blimps escorted transport convoys and assisted the escort carrier groups in hunting German U-Boats. These airships often landed aboard escort carriers to take on fuel, supplies, and ordnance. Blimps were armed with depth charges and bombs. (Real War Photos)

A US Army Air Forces Sikorsky R-4B Hoverfly (43-46582) takes off from an escort carrier during a feasibility test in 1944. The R-4 was camouflaged in the standard Olive Drab over Neutral Gray scheme for early helicopters. This Hoverfly was fitted with air-inflated floats, which allowed the helicopter to land on either water or hard surfaces. An XR-4 prototype made the first helicopter landing on a ship at sea aboard the merchant tanker BUNKER HILL on 7 May 1943. During World War Two, the US Navy received seven R-4Bs (redesignated HNS-1s) for training and air/sea rescue duties. (Real War Photos)

Crewmen prepare to launch a target drone from an escort carrier during 1944. The drone controller crouched aft of the tail while adjusting the drone's radio controller prior to engine start. The remote-controlled target was launched from the ship's catapult and guided to fly near the carrier. The US Navy used target drones to train anti-aircraft gunners. Drones were made of non-essential materials, since they were expendable. This drone was painted in a high visibility scheme of Bright Red (FS31136), with Orange Yellow (FS33538) wings. (Real War Photos)

Captured Mitsubishi A6M Zero (Allied codename Zeke) fighters are spotted on the aft flight deck of USS COPAHEE (CVE-12) on 10 July 1944. Some of these aircraft retained their Japanese national insignia. Allied Forces intelligence officers in the US received the captured Zeroes delivered by this ship for testing and evaluation. The tests determined if anything of value could be learned from the aircraft. It is believed the Zeroes were test flown by US pilots to determine their capabilities. Information gathered by Allied intelligence on the A6M's strengths and weaknesses was then passed on to Allied pilots. This information was also shared with aircraft and armament manufacturers, whose products were intended to counter the Zero. (Real War Photos)

Ensign Darrell C. Bennett of VC-10 stands beside the nose of his FM-2 (27) aboard the escort carrier GAMBIER BAY (CVE-73) on 1 August 1944. Smokey's Lucky Witch portrayed two lovely portraits of womanhood on the cowl. The forward 'pin up' was a common nose art on US fighters and bombers in both the European and Pacific theaters of war. This individual design was one of the most blatant examples of disregarding US Navy orders against nose art on aircraft. The original aircraft number 13 was painted out in favor of the new number, 27. The Wildcat was camouflaged in the three-tone scheme of Sea Blue, Intermediate Blue, and White. Bennett is wearing his AN-H-15 cloth helmet on his head, with his goggles resting on the helmet. He also wears a khaki shirt and trousers, rather than the standard one-piece khaki flight suit normally worn by US Navy pilots in the Pacific. Ens. Bennett holds his 'Mae West' inflatable life vest in his right hand. The vest was normally worn over his chest for overwater flights. The Japanese super battleship YAMATO sank GAMBIER BAY off Samar in the Philippines on 25 October 1944. (National Archives)

Eastern Aircraft FM-2 Wildcat

Catapult crews secure a VC-36 TBF-1C (8) for launch from MISSION BAY (CVE-59) on 14 September 1944. The catapult bridle was placed onto hooks attached to the Avenger's main landing gear doors. The CASABLANCA class escort carrier MISSION BAY operated in the South Atlantic while hunting German U-Boats. The TBF-1C was camouflaged in the Atlantic aircraft scheme of Dark Gull Gray (FS36231) over Nonspecular White (FS37875). (Real War Photos)

(Above) A TBM-3 (7, *Miss-Behaving*) prepares to launch from the starboard catapult of USS INDEPENDENCE (CVL-22) on 10 October 1944. A TBM-1D (23) was just launched from the port catapult. This aircraft was fitted with a radar antenna pod on the starboard wing for night attacks. Both TBMs were believed to be assigned to VT-46 aboard INDEPENDENCE, the lead ship of a class of nine light carriers. The Avengers were finished in overall Glossy Sea Blue (FS15042), which the US Navy authorized for all carrier-based aircraft on 7 October 1944. (Real War Photos)

(Right) Ordnancemen dolly and carry 5 inch (12.7 CM) High Velocity Air Rockets (HVARs) down the flight deck of HANCOCK (CV-19) on 12 October 1944. The rocket dolly was modified from a bomb carrier, which expedited delivery of the 140 pound (63.5 KG) rockets to the aircraft. HANCOCK's aircraft were prepared to raid the Japanese occupied island of Formosa (now Taiwan). The HVAR was nicknamed the 'Holy Moses' by US sailors and airmen because of the fire that streamed from the tail when it was launched. (National Archives)

A Curtiss SB2C-3 Helldiver (58) assigned to VB-15 folds its wings after recovering aboard ESSEX in October of 1944. The starboard horizontal stabilizer was slightly damaged by Japanese fire. The white vertical stabilizer band identified the ESSEX air group. Deck crewmen directed the Helldiver to the forward flight deck to make room for more incoming aircraft. (Via Jim Sullivan)

45

Ordnancemen – including some wearing Army-style steel helmets – arm VT-51 TBM-1 torpedo bombers aboard the light carrier SAN JACINTO (CVL-30) on 25 October 1944. The Avengers were readied to attack Japanese carrier forces off Cape Engano, northeast of the Philippines. Plywood water-entry shrouds covered the Mk 13 torpedo's nose and tail fins. These shrouds improved the weapon's stability when released from the aircraft and broke away once the torpedo hit the water. The near TBM (1) had an Orange Yellow propeller spinner tip and band. (National Archives)

A VF-80 F6F-3 taxis up to the starboard catapult of USS TICONDEROGA (CV-14) in October of 1944. The Hellcat is camouflaged in the overall Glossy Sea Blue scheme first authorized for US Navy fighters on 13 March 1944. This scheme was adopted for all carrier-based aircraft from 7 October 1944. The F6F was fitted with a 150 gallon (567.8 L) extended range fuel tank on the centerline. Three sets of Mk V zero length rocket launchers were mounted under each wing for carrying 5 inch HVARs on ground attack missions. (Floating Drydock)

Ordnancemen load incendiary bombs in the bomb bay of a VT-20 TBM-1C aboard ENTERPRISE (CV-6) in October of 1944. This weapon consisted of a cluster of white phosphorous rods, which burst into flame on contact with the air. The Avenger was armed for raids on Japanese positions on the Philippine island of Leyte. The TBM's bomb bay held a maximum of 2000 pounds (907.2 KG) of bombs and other ordnance. SB2C Helldivers of VB-20 were spotted ahead of the TBM. (Real War Photos)

A VC-79 F6F-3 launches from the port side catapult of the escort carrier SARGENT BAY (CVE-83) on 30 October 1944. The Hellcat was directed to cover re-supply operations in the Philippines. F6Fs usually were not assigned to Composite Squadrons complement on the small escort carriers, due to space constraints. FM (Eastern Aircraft-built F4F) Wildcats were the preferred fighters for the CVEs, with the US Navy assigning most F6Fs to the fleet and light carriers. The F6F was fitted with a 150 gallon extended range fuel tank under the fuselage. (Real War Photos)

A *kamikaze* ('divine wind' suicide aircraft) attacked the light carrier BELLEAU WOOD (CVL-24) on 30 October 1944, hitting the ship on the aft flight deck. The carrier was operating off of the Philippines when she was hit. Flight deck crewmen moved undamaged TBM-1 torpedo bombers and F6F-3 fighters away from the flames, while shipmates fought the fires. The fleet carrier FRANKLIN (CV-13), also hit during the same attack, burns in the distance off BELLEAU WOOD's port quarter. The light carrier was repaired in the United States and returned to the Pacific war zone three months after the attack. (National Archives)

A North American PBJ-1H (B-25H) Mitchell, modified with a tail hook, makes a successful arrested landing aboard SHANGRI-LA (CV-38) in November of 1944. The PBJ was used to test the suitability of large tricycle gear equipped aircraft on carrier decks. The PBJ (B-25) was no stranger to the carrier deck, since this was the same aircraft type that flew off of the imaginary 'Shangri-La' (HORNET, CV-8) to attack Japan in April of 1942. The US Marines operated PBJs in land-based bombing roles in the southwest Pacific during World War Two. (Via Jim Sullivan)

This VF-29 F6F-3 (25) required the crash barrier to recover aboard INTREPID in November of 1944. Japanese anti-aircraft fire damaged the Hellcat's starboard flap and fuselage side. The wire radio antenna stretched from the mid-fuselage radio mast to the top of the vertical stabilizer also sustained damage. Deck crewmen removed the barrier cables that entangled the F6F's propeller and landing gear. The aircraft required considerable work from airframe and engine mechanics before it was returned to service. INTREPID's vertical white bar insignia was painted on the F6F's tail. (Via Jim Sullivan)

A VC-79 TBM-1C (19), piloted by Lt. (jg) D. E. Sheiver, bounces off the flight deck while engaging an arresting cable aboard SARGENT BAY on 11 November 1944. The Avenger returned to the escort carrier with eight 5 inch HVARs under the wings, which indicated these rockets were not fired on the mission. ASB radar antennas were mounted on the outboard wing undersurfaces. The TBM was finished in the three-tone (Sea Blue, Intermediate Blue, and White) color scheme. A supply ship steamed off SARGENT BAY's port quarter. (Real War Photos)

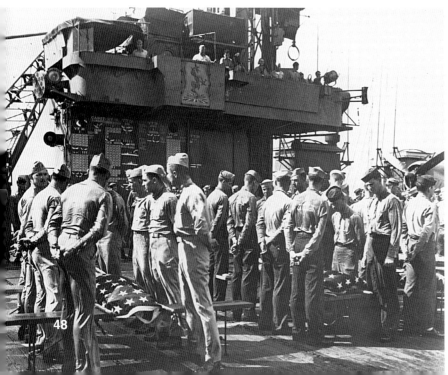

Officers and sailors prepare to bury two comrades lost aboard USS CABOT (CVL-28) on 14 November 1944. The INDEPENDENCE class light carrier was hit during a *kamikaze* attack off Leyte in the Philippine Islands, which killed 62 crewmen. The bodies of US sailors killed at sea were placed inside canvas shrouds. A heavy object was placed inside the shroud to ensure the body would sink into the sea floor. American flags were draped over the shrouds for the funeral ceremony, which concluded with the bodies tipped overboard. This funeral was held beside CABOT's island superstructure. The ship's mascot was painted on an area aft of the bridge. Scoreboards for the carrier's squadrons – VF-29, VF-31, VT-29, and VT-31 – were placed along the lower superstructure side, below the bridge. CABOT was repaired at Ulithi Atoll in the Carolines and resumed operations in December of 1944. (Floating Drydock)

A Grumman F7F-1 Tigercat launches without catapult assistance during carrier suitability trials on SHANGRI-LA in November of 1944. The F7F was the US Navy's first operational twin engine fighter and the service's first carrier-based aircraft with a tricycle landing gear. The Tigercat arrived too late for service in the Pacific War; however, the US Marines flew night fighter variants during the Korean War (1950-1953). The aircraft carried no markings except for the national insignia and the finish is overall Glossy Sea Blue. (Via Jim Sullivan)

The deck officer waves his black and white checkered flag in the take-off signal to an SB2C-3 Helldiver (1) aboard HANCOCK (CV-19) on 25 November 1944. He wore a yellow long-sleeved shirt for greater visibility on the flight deck. The VB-7 aircraft was launched to attack Japanese shipping and installations in Manila Bay, Philippines. The SB2C's propeller spinner and cowl lip were white and the aircraft was fitted with a 58 gallon (219.6 L) fuel tank on the starboard wing pylon. (National Archives)

A TBM Avenger uses Rocket Assisted Take Off (RATO) units and catapult to launch from MAKASSAR STRAIT (CVE-91) in late 1944. Two RATO units were mounted on the lower aft fuselage and fired when the aircraft began its catapult launch. RATO enabled the Avenger to take off while fully loaded without using a catapult – even from the decks of small escort carriers. Although this test was successful, the advantages of RATO launches were insufficient for this to become a fleet standard. RATO units were not required for deck use when more powerful steam catapult replaced hydraulic catapults in the early 1950s. (Real War Photos)

1945 – Final Victory

The year 1945 proved to be the end for the forces of Nazi Germany in Europe and Imperial Japan in the Pacific. Although decimated by years of Allied attacks, the Axis forces still had some fight in them and would fight to the bitter end to defend their respective homelands.

On 3 January, US forces invaded the principal Philippine Island of Luzon. Seventh Fleet escort carriers directly supported by the fast carrier forces of Task Force 38[1] provided air cover for the amphibious forces. The *kamikaze* (suicide aircraft) were out in force and some were able to penetrate the Combat Air Patrol (CAP). *Kamikazes* sank the escort carrier **OMMANEY BAY** (CVE-79) off Lingayen on 4 January and damaged **MANILA BAY** (CVE-61) and **SAVO ISLAND** (CVE-78) the next day. Luzon was finally secured on 3 March after fierce battles – particularly for the Philippine capital, Manila – which cost nearly 8000 American lives.

US Marines assaulted Iwo Jima in the Bonin Islands on 19 February, with Task Force 58 carrier aircraft providing air support. During one month of air attacks in the Iwo Jima area, US Navy aircraft destroyed 648 Japanese aircraft and sank 30,000 tons of merchant shipping. The Japanese response was again to employ the kamikaze against the carrier forces, sinking the escort carrier **BISMARCK SEA** (CVE-95) and damaging SARATOGA (CV-3) on 21 January.

On 18 March, US carrier aircraft began striking Japanese positions in the southernmost home island of Kyushu. These raids were designed to soften Japanese defenses before the US invaded the island of Okinawa, located approximately 350 miles (563.3 KM) south of the Japanese home islands. The *kamikaze* were out again in force employing bombs, aircraft, and the new rocket-powered Kugisho **MXY7 *Ohka*** (Allied codename **Baka**) piloted flying bomb against the Allied fleet. A bomber attacked and seriously damaged the fleet carrier **FRANKLIN** (CV-13)

off the Japanese coast on 19 March. She had to sail back to New York for extensive repairs; however, FRANKLIN would never sail in harm's way again. The amphibious assault on Okinawa (Operation ICEBERG) began on 1 April and fighting continued until US forces secured the island on 21 June. It was the last island attacked by American amphibious forces during the Pacific War. During the Okinawa campaign, attacks by 1465 *kamikaze* aircraft damaged over ten American carriers and numerous other warships. The ferocity of these suicide attacks increased the closer US naval forces came to Japan. The *kamikaze* attacks were one of the major factors in the US decision to drop the atomic bomb on Hiroshima on 6 August 1945.

The war in Europe ended with Germany's surrender on 8 May 1945. This enabled the Allied forces to concentrate solely on the war in the Pacific. On 10 July, 14 US carriers began concentrated attacks on the Japanese home islands, from Kyushu in the south to Hokkaido in the north. Six days later, the British deployed four carriers in air attacks on Japan. This final carrier assault destroyed over 1200 Japanese aircraft and sank 23 warships and 48 merchant ships totaling 290,000 tons.

Carrier forces were withdrawn from the Japanese coast in early August, after the decision was made to drop the first atomic bomb. This redeployment was due to concern over the new weapon's actual effect, which was unknown. On 6 August, a US Army Air Forces **B-29 Superfortress** dropped the first atomic bomb on Hiroshima. The second atomic bomb was dropped on the industrial city of Nagasaki on 9 August, an event that finally sealed the fate of the Imperial Japanese forces. Japan agreed to an unconditional surrender on 14 August. The formal instrument of surrender was signed aboard the battleship **USS MISSOURI** (BB-63) in Tokyo Bay on 2 September 1945.

US carrier aviation played a major role in the defeat of the Japanese and German aggressors in World War Two. The three and one half-year conflict for the American Naval forces proved the worth of the large fleet carriers, the light carriers, and the small escort carriers.

[1]The fast carrier task force was designated Task Force 38 (TF 38) when it was under the Third Fleet, the Central Pacific Force commanded by Adm. William F. 'Bull' Halsey, Jr. TF 38 was redesignated Task Force 58 (TF 58) when the Third Fleet became the Fifth Fleet under Adm. Raymond A. Spruance. The Fleets remained the same; only the designations changed with the change in command.

A VC-8 FM-2 Wildcat (2) sustained damage to its port aileron from Japanese fire, but safely recovered aboard MAKIN ISLAND (CVE-93) on 1 January 1945. Deck crewmen arrived to fold the Wildcat's wings and direct the aircraft towards its spot on the forward flight deck. The aircraft was overall Glossy Sea Blue (FS15042), with the national insignia in Insignia Blue (FS15045) and White (FS17875). Engine exhaust staining followed the wing camber (curvature) as it trailed aft along the fuselage. The FM-2's tail stripe and propeller spinner were Orange Yellow (FS13538), while the aircraft number was White. (Real War Photos)

A TBM-1C (5) assigned to VC-84 is catapulted off the MAKIN ISLAND's deck on 8 January 1945. The aircraft was Nonspecular Sea Blue (FS35045), Intermediate Blue (FS35164), and Nonspecular White (FS37875). An Orange Yellow tail band identifying the carrier was painted across the vertical tail. The catapult bridle immediately below the TBM was restrained by a cable attached to the flight deck. This allowed the bridle to be used again. The catapult operator stood alongside the flight deck, just below the Avenger's tail while the aircraft passed. A twin mounted 40MM Bofors anti-aircraft cannon was placed in the catwalk near the carrier's bow. (Real War Photos)

A 2000 pound (907.2 KG) general-purpose bomb sits on a bomb dolly on the deck of HOGGATT BAY (CVE-75) on 8 January 1945. The weapon was marked with 'well wishes' in chalk for the Japanese intended to receive it. The bomb was hauled on the dolly to a VC-88 TBM-1, where the weapon was loaded into the bomb bay and fused. US aircraft bombs were painted overall Olive Drab (FS34087). An Orange Yellow ring around the aft body indicated a high explosive weapon. (Real War Photos)

The tail hook of this VF-16 F6F-5P Hellcat (99) engages the number three cable while its landing gear snares the number five barrier on BON HOMME RICHARD (CV-31) on 16 January 1945. ESSEX class fleet carriers were usually equipped with 15 arresting cables and five crash barriers; they were numbered from bow to stern. The F6F-5P was a standard F6F-5 fighter modified by the US Navy for the reconnaissance role. This aircraft appeared to have the aerial camera field mounted on the starboard side of the fuselage, aft and below the canopy. Cameras were normally installed on the port fuselage side. The Hellcat was overall Glossy Sea Blue. (Real War Photos)

A VC-84 FM-2 Wildcat (14) takes a wave off while attempting to recover aboard MAKIN ISLAND in early 1945. The Landing Signal Officer (LSO), who waved off the Wildcat, crouches on the flight deck's edge. The Assistant LSO looked from behind the canvas windshield forward of the LSO's station. The tail hook extended from the fighter's tail section. Two 58 gallon (219.6 L) fuel tanks were fitted under the FM-2's wings. An Orange Yellow air group identification band appeared on the vertical stabilizer. (National Archives)

The catapult officer prepares to order the launch of a VF-6 F6F-3 (22) from HANCOCK (CV-19) on 2 February 1945. The catapult bridle was fitted between the Hellcat's wings and the catapult shuttle. This fighter was fitted with a 150 gallon (567.8 L) centerline fuel tank, which retained the old Nonspecular White undersurface color scheme. The tank was usually jettisoned when the F6F encountered enemy aircraft. The Hellcat was finished in overall Glossy Sea Blue, with a White propeller spinner and tail band. The gun ports on the wing's leading edge were taped over to keep foreign objects from the ports. The tape also slightly increased the aircraft's performance, through streamlining of this wing section. (Real War Photos)

Four ordnancemen – one partially hidden by the weapon – load a 250 pound (113.4 KG) general-purpose bomb onto the port wing pylon of a SB2C-4 (102) on 7 February 1945. They lifted the weapon from the bomb cart to the pylon by hand, instead of using a bomb hoist. Ordnancemen wore red shirts with dark blue trousers, but appear to be wearing a variety of shoes. The Helldiver was assigned to VB-3 aboard YORKTOWN (CV-10). Aircraft number 102 was black on the main landing gear door and white on the wing leading edge, beside the 20MM cannon barrel. The dive-bomber was finished in the three-tone color scheme. (Real War Photos)

A 500 pound (226.8 KG) general-purpose bomb is loaded onto a VT-86 TBM-1C, *John* (309) aboard WASP (CV-18). This Avenger was among the US carrier-based aircraft that raided Tokyo on 16 February 1945. Deck crewmen wore rain gear – water-repellant hooded jackets and trousers – to stay dry during inclement weather. The TBM retained the three-tone camouflage scheme, while the F6F Hellcat parked to port is overall Glossy Sea Blue. The white number on the cowl (309) appeared to have been painted over a former number assigned to this Avenger. (Real War Photos)

Deck crew and ordnancemen with 5 inch (12.7 CM) High Velocity Air Rockets (HVARs) dash across the flight deck aboard SARGENT BAY (CVE-83) on 16 February 1945. They were heading from the FM-2 Wildcats of VC-79, which were spotted along the port edge of the deck. The Wildcats were armed with four HVARs and were fitted with 58 gallon fuel tanks under the wings. VC-79's FM-2s were launched to attack Japanese targets on Iwo Jima, which was invaded by US forces three days later. (Real War Photos)

An F4U-1D Corsair (114) from Fighter-Bomber Squadron Eighty Six (VFB-86) prepares to launch from WASP's slicked flight deck on 16 February 1945. The fighter was sent to attack Japanese targets around Tokyo, diverting attention from the impending invasion of Iwo Jima. The Corsair was fitted with a 155 gallon (586.7 L) extended range fuel tank under the starboard wing and a 500 pound general purpose bomb to port. (Real War Photos)

A Grumman F8F-1 Bearcat warms up its engine before launching from USS CHARGER (CVE-30) on 17 February 1945. The Bearcat was deployed to the escort carrier for carrier qualification and suitability trials prior to it entering fleet squadron service. The aircraft was painted overall Glossy Sea Blue, which was authorized for all US carrier aircraft in June of 1944. The national insignia's white star and bars were painted directly on the Glossy Sea Blue surface, without an Insignia Blue disc and trim. The F8F Bearcat – like its Grumman stablemate, the F7F Tigercat – entered service too late to see combat against Japan in the Pacific. (Floating Drydock)

A VF-3 F6F-5 Hellcat (37) prepares to launch from YORKTOWN on 17 February 1945. The Hellcat was armed with six 5-inch HVARs for ground attack. A 150 gallon centerline fuel tank was fitted to the Hellcat, allowing for longer range and endurance. The F6F was overall Glossy Sea Blue with White markings, including the tail design. This design was unique to YORKTOWN's air group and was among the distinct geometric patterns adopted for Pacific fleet carriers on 27 January 1945. (Via Jim Sullivan)

An F6F-3 (60) assigned to VF-82 is about to launch from BENNINGTON (CV-20) in February of 1945. This was one of the aircraft dispatched for the first carrier strikes against targets in and around Tokyo. An upward pointing arrowhead identified BENNINGTON's air group. This design was painted on the rudder, the upper starboard aileron, and the lower port aileron. A 150-gallon fuel tank was mounted on the centerline. Another aircraft, previously launched from this carrier, is in the background. (Real War Photos)

The pilot of this VF-3 F6F-3 (2) crashed his Hellcat into a barrier while recovering aboard YORK-TOWN on 17 February 1945. He is exiting the cockpit and stepping onto the starboard wing. The crash crew extended a ladder onto the wing to assist the pilot in evacuating the aircraft. Other crewmen watched the aircraft in case of a fire – the most feared occurrence on the flight deck. The F6F's engine quickly stopped after the aircraft landed on its nose. Mechanics later inspected the Hellcat for damage from the mishap. (Real War Photos)

A Japanese bomb has just hit the forward flight deck of SARATOGA (CV-3) on 17 February 1945. The weapon destroyed an F6F-5N assigned to Fighting Squadron (Night) Fifty Three (VF(N)-53). Another Hellcat parked alongside the F6F-5N was slightly damaged, while a third Hellcat (7) kept its engine running. This fighter was waiting its turn on the starboard side catapult when the bomb struck. SARATOGA was operating off Iwo Jima when conventional and *kamikaze* aircraft attacked her. She was repaired in the United States before being redeployed in pilot training for the remainder of the Pacific War. SARATOGA's aircraft were marked with a white chevron on the vertical tail and upper starboard and lower port wingtips. (Via Jim Sullivan)

Lt. Henry F. Rowland inspects the damage to the rudder of his VF-3 F6F-3 aboard YORKTOWN on 17 February 1945. Japanese anti-aircraft fire shot through the fabric covering and one of the metal ribs. Rowland was able to safely recover his Hellcat aboard YORKTOWN, despite this damage. Another pilot returns safely to his carrier aboard a sturdy aircraft from the Grumman 'Iron Works.' (Real War Photos)

55

A naval aviator crashed his F4U-1D Corsair against the island of the escort training carrier PRINCE WILLIAM (CVE-31) on 24 February 1945. The aircraft caught fire and its starboard wing ended up in the starboard catwalk. Emergency damage control personnel prepare to apply fire suppressant foam on the burning Corsair. The F4U appears to have buckled at the cockpit; it is unknown if the pilot survived this crash. The BOGUE class escort carrier PRINCE WILLIAM was used for carrier pilot training and aircraft transport duties in the Atlantic from mid-1944 until mid-1945. (Real War Photos)

A VT-82 TBM-3 (110) prepares to launch from the wet deck of BENNINGTON in February of 1945. The AN-A6 gun camera mounted ahead of aircraft 110's windshield recorded the results of the raid on targets in and around Tokyo. VT-82 was a designated torpedo squadron; however, this unit and other VTs were primarily used to bomb land targets during the last months of the Pacific War. This was due to the scarcity of Japanese naval targets during this period. (Real War Photos)

A TBM-1C from VC-79 is positioned on the port side catapult aboard SARGENT BAY on 19 February 1945. The Avenger was soon launched to hit Japanese targets on Iwo Jima in support of the US invasion that day. The catapult officer brought the aircraft forward, which allowed the catapult crew to attach the catapult bridle to hooks mounted on the main landing gear. The Avenger is fitted with an AN-A6 gun camera immediately forward of the windshield. (Real War Photos)

F4U-1D and Goodyear Aircraft FG-1D Corsairs from VF-84 and Marine Fighting Squadron Two Twenty One (VMF-221) taxi forward to launch positions aboard BUNKER HILL (CV-17) in February of 1945. The lead aircraft (152) has just received the take off flag from Fly-One (lead flight deck officer) and will soon launch from the ship. Orange Yellow cowl rings identified US aircraft on the raid against targets on Kyushu, one of the Japanese home islands. BUNKER HILL's aircraft were marked with white upward-pointing arrows on the vertical tail surfaces. (Via Jim Sullivan)

A VF-84 F4U-1D (187) takes off from BUNKER HILL's moist flight deck to attack targets on Kyushu in February of 1945. The Corsair was marked with the ship's familiar 'this side up' emblem on the vertical stabilizer and starboard wing upper surface. This insignia was also painted on the port wing undersurface. The Corsair was overall Glossy Sea Blue with national markings in White and Insignia Blue. White 'markings' immediately forward of the windshield were actually tape used to seal the main fuel tank cover. Fuel leaks and cockpit vapors were a problem on F4U-1s. (Real War Photos)

A battle scarred VC-79 TBM (027) is about to be launched from SARGENT BAY's port catapult on 25 February 1945. All valuable parts – including the engine – were stripped from the airframe; these parts were made available to repair other TBMs aboard the carrier. Numerous holes were cut into the fuselage to ensure its rapid sinking before the ship's bow reaches the site. Limited space aboard aircraft carriers resulted in heavily damaged aircraft usually being jettisoned overboard. (Real War Photos)

An FM-2 (15) assigned to VC-88 has just landed aboard the escort carrier HOGGATT BAY in March of 1945. A deck crewman directs the pilot to taxi forward on the flight deck, allowing room for other landing aircraft. The Wildcat was overall Glossy Sea Blue with two white aft fuselage bands. The forward band was painted over the Insignia Blue portion of the national insignia. The area under the horizontal stabilizer was also white. The upper starboard and lower port wings of HOGGATT BAY's aircraft were marked with two white bands and a white rectangular patch outboard of the bands. These markings were designed to aid aircraft spotters in distinguishing friendly aircraft from foes. VC-88's impressive scoreboard was painted on the side of the bridge. (Floating Drydock)

A Landing Signal Officer (LSO) directs an aircraft for landing aboard MAKASSAR STRAIT (CVE-91) in 1945. The LSO brought the aircraft in by having the pilot mimic the signals that are given to him; in this instance, the LSO wanted the pilot to lower his port wing to get in the 'groove' (correct glide path) for recovery. A spotter (usually the Assistant LSO) would have already determined that the flaps, landing gear, and tail hook were lowered. This information would be called out to the LSO. He had the decision to either authorize the pilot to cut his engine and land, or wave off the pilot and have him go around to make another recovery attempt. (Real War Photos)

The LSO gives the pilot of this TBM-1C the 'cut engine' signal prior to the Avenger landing aboard TAKANSIS BAY (CVE-89) on 18 March 1945. There were many different styles of paddles used by the LSOs, but most were constructed of brightly colored cloth to increase visibility for the pilot. A plane guard destroyer cruised off the carrier's stern, ready to pick up any survivors of aircraft that crashed into the sea during flight operations. (Real War Photos)

F4U-1D and FG-1D (Goodyear-built F4U-1D) Corsairs crowd the forward flight deck of HANCOCK on 21 March 1945. These aircraft were assigned to VBF-6 and VF-6. Some Corsairs – believed to be from VBF-6 – were fitted with 5 inch rockets under the wings. The warheads were not fitted to the rockets at that time; these were installed prior to launch. HANCOCK's two forward 5 inch twin gun turrets were mounted ahead of the island superstructure. These weapons were used primarily in the anti-aircraft role, although they were capable of engaging surface targets. (Via Jim Sullivan)

Ordnancemen prepare an SB2C-5's bomb crutch to receive a 1500 pound (680.4 KG) armor piercing bomb aboard WASP in March of 1945. The Helldiver was assigned to VB-86, which was tasked to raid Japanese naval targets. The bomb was fitted to the crutch, which retracted into the bomb bay. The crutch was extended when the bay doors were opened and swung the bomb below the propeller blade arc at high dive angles. This crutch was also a feature of earlier US Navy dive-bombers, including the SBC Helldiver, the SB2U Vindicator, and the SBD Dauntless. (Real War Photos)

Curtiss SB2C-5 Helldiver

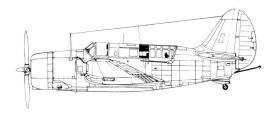

Armorers feed ammunition belts to the starboard wing .50 caliber machine guns on an F6F-3 aboard ESSEX (CV-9) on 27 March 1945. The Hellcat was assigned to VF-4, the 'Red Rippers.' The F6F was armed with six wing-mounted .50 caliber Browning M2 machine guns. Each weapon had an ammunition capacity of 400 rounds. The air group insignia for ESSEX was hastily applied, with considerable overspray of the white paint onto the Glossy Sea Blue overall airframe finish. (Real War Photos).

Armorers load 5 inch High Velocity Air Rockets (HVARs) onto a VBF-83 F4U-1D (182) aboard ESSEX on 27 March 1945. The rocket bodies were installed on zero length launch rails on the wing undersurfaces. The projectiles were then attached to the rocket. This separation of rocket bodies and projectiles was a safety measure. Each Corsair carried six HVARs under its wings. A salvo of all six rockets firing at once equaled the broadside of a destroyer. (Real War Photos)

A VBF-6 F4U-1D (28) is moved off the amidships deck edge elevator of HANCOCK on 21 March 1945. The ESSEX class carriers were equipped with three aircraft elevators – forward, amidships, and aft. The forward and aft elevators were within the flight deck, while the deck edge elevator could be folded upwards to allow the ship's passage through the Panama Canal. Aircraft were transferred between the flight deck and the hangar deck using the elevators. The overall Glossy Sea Blue aircraft had the carrier's white diagonal stripe painted on the vertical tail. The cowl front was painted white, although the edge dividing this from the Glossy Sea Blue was ragged. (Via Jim Sullivan)

An F6F-5 (50) from VF-6 is hooked up on the port catapult on the escort carrier SUWANNEE (CVE-27) on 20 April 1945. The catapult officer prepares to signal for launch, while the Hellcat's pilot braces in his seat for the sudden acceleration of a catapult launch. A 150 gallon fuel tank was fitted on the F6F's centerline. The color scheme was Glossy Sea blue with white markings. VF-6 was normally assigned to HANCOCK, but cross decked (transferred) to SUWANNEE. This allowed HANCOCK to retire for repairs following a *kamikaze* attack on 7 April 1945. (Via Jim Sullivan)

A VC-88 FM-2 Wildcat (A1) is hooked up to the catapult bridle prior to launching from SAGINAW BAY (CVE-82) in the spring of 1945. This Squadron provided fighter cover for the US invasion of Okinawa (Operation ICEBERG), which began on 1 April 1945. The Wildcat was camouflaged in the three tone color scheme: Sea Blue upper surfaces, Intermediate Blue sides, White undersurfaces. Heavy exhaust staining from the FM-2's engine discolored the forward fuselage. (Real War Photos)

A US Marine Stinson (Consolidated-built) OY-1 Sentinel launches off of the escort carrier SANGAMON (CVE-26) to provide forward air control duties. The light aircraft became airborne in a short distance, using the wind coming over the flight deck and the carrier's speed to aid in the take off. The OY-1 was the Marine version of the Army L-5 light aircraft, which was used to direct artillery, perform liaison duties, and rescue downed airmen. The OY-1 was camouflaged in an Olive Drab (FS34087) and Sand (FS30279) over Neutral Gray (FS36173) scheme. (Real War Photos)

Deck crewmen tow an F4U-1D into position aboard BUNKER HILL. The Corsair was spotted with other aircraft from VF-84, VBF-84, VMF-251, and VMF-451. BUNKER HILL's air group was equipped with F4U-1D and FG-1D Corsairs, F6F-5 Hellcats, and SB2C-5 Helldivers. The aircraft were spotted on the aft flight deck prior to a raid on Kyushu in the spring of 1945. All aircraft, except for the Helldivers, had Orange Yellow cowl nose bands. These bands identified friendly aircraft to US fighters flying in the vicinity. (Via Jim Sullivan)

Deck crewman repair damage to the flight deck of USS ANTI-ETAM (CV-36) on 6 April 1945. This was made necessary when an F4U-1D Corsair crash landed while recovering aboard the ESSEX class carrier, which was making its shakedown cruise. Armorers remove .50 caliber ammunition from the Corsair's six machine guns so the aircraft could be moved using the aircraft handling crane. The crane was mounted on a wheeled base for easy movement anywhere along the flight deck. It was believed the wood flight deck was gouged by the F4U's propeller while it crash landed. (Real War Photos)

A pilot starts deplaning from a VF(N)-52 F7F-2N Tigercat (23) after recovering aboard ANTIETAM on 8 April 1945. A 150 gallon fuel tank was fitted to the aircraft centerline. The night fighter squadron conducted a carrier qualification exercise with the carrier off Trinidad in the Caribbean Sea. Six VF(N)-52 pilots were qualified for day/night operations with the Tigercat at sea. The F7F-2N was overall Glossy Sea Blue, with a white number on the cowl. (Real War Photos)

Grumman F7F-2N Tigercat

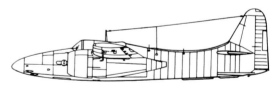

A TBM-1C (84) makes an emergency landing aboard ANTIETAM on 9 April 1945. It was believed the Avenger's Pratt & Whitney R-2600 engine had either blown a cylinder or lost oil through some malfunction. The emergency crew quickly responded with fire extinguishers and foam to put out any fires. ANTIETAM did not see action during World War Two, only deploying to the western Pacific just after the war ended. (Real War Photos)

An FM-2 (M3) requires the crash barrier to land aboard the training carrier SABLE (IX-81) in May of 1945. The Wildcat was unable to engage any of the carrier's arresting cables with its tail hook. There was little apparent damage to the aircraft following this incident. SABLE was the paddle wheel steamer GREATER BUFFALO converted to an aircraft carrier. A flight deck was installed atop the passenger liner's hull. SABLE was commissioned on 8 March 1943 and used Chicago as its home port. She sailed the Great Lakes training naval aviators and deck crew for the remainder of the war. A number of carrier aircraft have been recovered from the cold, fresh waters of the Great Lakes and are under restoration. (National Archives)

An F4U-1D (EE55) from VMF-512 is hooked up prior to being catapulted from USS GILBERT ISLANDS (CVE-107) on 10 May 1945. The hold back bar was placed between the deck and the tail wheel. GILBERT ISLANDS was the second carrier to host all-Marine squadrons onboard. (The first was its sister ship, BLOCK ISLAND [CVE-106].) VMF-512 participated in the invasion of Okinawa, which began on 1 April 1945. US forces secured the island after fierce combat with Japanese forces on 21 June. (Real War Photos)

Damage control crewmen aboard ENTERPRISE (CV-6) respond to a *kamikaze* attack on the carrier on 14 May 1945. A Japanese suicide aircraft burst through the defenses and crashed into the forward elevator. An F6F-5N from VF(N)-90 was severely damaged and was likely jettisoned overboard. This attack caused ENTERPRISE to withdraw from action for the remainder of World War Two. The carrier earned 20 Battle Stars for her service in the Pacific, which began with the Japanese attack on Pearl Harbor on 7 December 1941. ENTERPRISE was away from Pearl Harbor when the Japanese raided the base; however, several of her SBDs were hit by Japanese fighters and US anti-aircraft fire over the base. (Real War Photos)

F5F-5 Hellcats from VF-12 and VFB-12 crowd the flight deck of RANDOLPH (CV-15) in June of 1945. The aircraft in the foreground straddle the number one through three cable arresting barriers. All these Hellcats were fitted with 150 gallon external fuel tanks under the fuselage, which increased the fighter's range and endurance. RANDOLPH's aircraft were marked with white upper starboard ailerons and white and Sea Blue stripes on the vertical tail. (Via Jim Sullivan)

SB2C-5s of VB-89 prepare to launch from ANTIETAM on 14 August 1945 – the day Japan agreed to surrender to the Allies. White stripes were painted on the upper aileron and vertical tail surfaces of the Helldivers assigned to this carrier. F4U-1D Corsairs were parked with their wings folded along the starboard side. ANTIETAM arrived in the Pacific Theater too late to see combat during the war. A FLETCHER class destroyer sailed across the carrier's bow to assume plane guard duty during the launching operation. (Real War Photos)